Congressional
Research
Service

The Federal Prison Population Buildup: Overview, Policy Changes, Issues, and Options

Nathan James
Analyst in Crime Policy

January 22, 2013

Congressional Research Service

7-5700

www.crs.gov

R42937

CRS Report for Congress ───────────────────────────

Prepared for Members and Committees of Congress

Summary

Since the early 1980s, there has been a historically unprecedented increase in the federal prison population. Some of the growth is attributable to changes in federal criminal justice policy during the previous three decades. An issue before Congress is whether policymakers consider the rate of growth in the federal prison population sustainable, and if not, what changes could be made to federal criminal justice policy to reduce the prison population while maintaining public safety. This report explores the issues related to the growing federal prison population.

The number of inmates under the Bureau of Prisons' (BOP) jurisdiction has increased from approximately 25,000 in FY1980 to nearly 219,000 in FY2012. Since FY1980, the federal prison population has increased, on average, by approximately 6,100 inmates each year. Data show that a growing proportion of inmates are being incarcerated for immigration- and weapons-related offenses, but the largest portion of newly admitted inmates are being incarcerated for drug offenses. Data also show that approximately 7 in 10 inmates are sentenced for five years or less.

Changes in federal sentencing and correctional policy since the early 1980s have contributed to the rapid growth in the federal prison population. These changes include increasing the number of federal offenses subject to mandatory minimum sentences; changes to the federal criminal code that have made more crimes federal offenses; and eliminating parole.

There are several issues related to the growing federal prison population that might be of interest to policymakers:

- The increasing number of federal inmates, combined with the rising per capita cost of incarceration, has made it increasingly more expensive to operate and maintain the federal prison system. The per capita cost of incarceration for all inmates increased from $19,571 in FY2000 to $26,094 in FY2011. During this same period of time, appropriations for the BOP increased from $3.668 billion to $6.381 billion.

- The federal prison system is increasingly overcrowded. Overall, the federal prison system was 39% over its rated capacity in FY2011, but high- and medium-security male facilities were operating at 51% and 55%, respectively, over rated capacity. At issue is whether overcrowding might lead to more inmate misconduct. The results of research on this topic have been mixed. One study found that overcrowding does not affect inmate misconduct; but the BOP, based on its own research, concluded that there is a significant positive relationship between the two.

- The inmate-to-staff ratio has increased from 4.1 inmates per staff member in FY2000 to 4.9 inmates per staff member in FY2011. Likewise, the inmate to correctional officer ratio increased from 9.8 inmates per correctional officer in FY2000 to 10.2 inmates per correctional officer in FY2011, but this is down from a high of 10.9 inmates per correctional officer in FY2005.

- The growing prison population is taking a toll on the infrastructure of the federal prison system. The BOP reports that it has a backlog of 154 modernization and repair projects with an approximate cost of $349 million for FY2012. Past appropriations left the BOP in a position where it could expand bedspace to manage overcrowding but not reduce it. However, reductions in funding since

FY2010 mean that the BOP will lack the funding to begin new prison construction in the near future. At the same time, it has become more expensive to expand the BOP's capacity.

Should Congress choose to consider policy options to address the issues resulting from the growth in the federal prison population, policymakers could choose options such as increasing the capacity of the federal prison system by building more prisons, investing in rehabilitative programming, or placing more inmates in private prisons.

Policymakers might also consider whether they want to revise some of the policy changes that have been made over the past three decades that have contributed to the steadily increasing number of offenders being incarcerated. For example, Congress could consider options such as (1) modifying mandatory minimum penalties, (2) expanding the use of Residential Reentry Centers, (3) placing more offenders on probation, (4) reinstating parole for federal inmates, (5) expanding the amount of good time credit an inmate can earn, and (6) repealing federal criminal statutes for some offenses.

Contents

Figures

Tables

Appendixes

Contacts

Introduction

The Bureau of Prisons (BOP) is the largest correctional agency in the country in terms of the number of prisoners under its jurisdiction.[1] The BOP currently operates 118 correctional facilities in 35 states and Puerto Rico.[2] The BOP was established in 1930 to house federal inmates, professionalize the prison service, and ensure consistent and centralized administration of the federal prison system.[3]

Since the early 1980s, there has been a historically unprecedented increase in the number of inmates incarcerated in the federal prison system. The number of inmates under the BOP's jurisdiction has increased from approximately 25,000 in FY1980 to nearly 219,000 in FY2012. In comparison, the federal prison population increased by approximately 12,000 inmates between 1930 and 1980. Since FY1980, the federal prison population has increased, on average, by approximately 6,100 inmates each fiscal year.

Some of the growth in the federal prison population is attributable to policy changes over the previous three decades, including

- increasing the number of federal offenses subject to mandatory minimum sentences,

- changes to the federal criminal code that have made more crimes federal offenses, and

- eliminating parole.

The BOP faces several challenges resulting from the increasing number of inmates placed under its supervision. The first is the increasing cost of operating the federal prison system. Data show that with each passing fiscal year it is increasingly more expensive to incarcerate an inmate in a federal prison, yet the BOP must operate the federal prison system within the annual appropriation approved by Congress. Second, the federal prison system is becoming more overcrowded, especially in high- and medium-security male prisons. Research conducted by the BOP suggests that there might be a link between higher levels of overcrowding and inmate misconduct. Third, the federal inmate population is increasing at a rate whereby the gap between the number of inmates and the number of staff and correctional officers is slowly starting to widen. Finally, the rising federal inmate population is starting to place a strain on the infrastructure of the federal prison system. The BOP has not been able to expand prison capacity at a rate that would allow it to close older prisons and it has also had to defer hundreds of millions of dollars in maintenance costs, which might result in either direct or indirect security problems.

There are a number of policy avenues lawmakers could consider should Congress choose to address the growth in the federal prison population. Several options—such as expanding the capacity of the federal prison system, continued investment in rehabilitative programs, and

---

[1] E. Ann Carson and William J. Sabol, *Prisoners in 2011*, U.S. Department of Justice, Office of Justice Programs, Bureau of Justice Statistics, NCJ 239808, Washington, DC, December 2012, p. 21, http://www.bjs.gov/content/pub/pdf/p11.pdf, hereinafter, *"Prisoners in 2011."*

[2] Data provided by the U.S. Department of Justice, Bureau of Prisons.

[3] U.S. Department of Justice, Bureau of Prisons, *About the Bureau of Prisons*, p. 1, http://www.bop.gov/about/index.jsp, hereinafter *"About the Bureau of Prisons."*

---

placing inmates in private prisons—either continue or expand current correctional policies. However, Congress might also consider changing some existing correctional or sentencing policies as a means of addressing some of the issues related to the growth of the federal prison population. Some of these options include placing some inmates in alternatives to incarceration, such as probation, or expanding early release options by allowing inmates to earn more good time credit or allowing inmates to be placed on parole once again. Congress could consider reducing the amount of time inmates are incarcerated in federal prisons by repealing mandatory minimum penalties for some offenses or reducing the length of the mandatory minimum sentence. Finally, policymakers could consider repealing federal criminal statutes for some offenses.

Federal Prison Population

At the end of 1930, the BOP operated 14 facilities that held approximately 13,000 inmates.[4] By the end of 1940, the BOP had expanded to 24 facilities that held approximately 24,000 inmates.[5] The number of inmates in the federal prison system, with a few fluctuations, remained at approximately 24,000 for the next four decades.[6] Then, as shown in **Figure 1**, beginning in FY1980 the federal prison population started an unabated, three-decade increase. The total number of inmates under the BOP's jurisdiction increased from approximately 25,000 in FY1980 to nearly 219,000 in FY2012. Between FY1980 and FY2012, the federal prison population increased, on average, by approximately 6,100 inmates annually. The growth in the federal prison population was much higher between FY1990 and FY2009 compared to the period of FY1980 through FY1989. On average, the federal prison population increased by approximately 3,700 inmates per fiscal year between FY1980 and FY1989. In contrast, the average increase per fiscal year between FY1990 and FY1999 was approximately 7,600 inmates and between FY2000 and FY2009 it was approximately 7,500 inmates. The growth in the federal prison population for the first few years of the current decade has been erratic. The federal prison population only grew by nearly 1,500 inmates between FY2009 and FY2010, but in FY2011, it grew by more than 7,500 inmates, which is more in line with previous trends. The total number of inmates in federal prison increased by approximately 900 prisoners in FY2012, the lowest level of annual growth in any fiscal year since FY1980.

Recent trends in the federal prison population stand in contrast to overall incarceration trends. The Bureau of Justice Statistics (BJS) reports that the total number of inmates under the jurisdiction of state correctional authorities decreased between 2009 (1,407,369) and 2010 (1,404,032) and between 2010 and 2011 (1,382,418).[7] However, while the number of state inmates has decreased, the federal prison population has continued to increase.

The data in **Figure 1** also show that most of the federal prison population is incarcerated in a BOP facility, as opposed to a contract facility.[8] However, over the years the BOP has had to rely increasingly on contract facilities to help manage the federal prison population. In FY1980, less

---

[4] U.S. Department of Justice, Bureau of Prisons, *A Brief History of the Bureau of Prisons*, http://www.bop.gov/about/history.jsp.

[5] Ibid.

[6] Ibid.

[7] *Prisoners in 2001*, p. 2.

[8] Contract facilities include bedspace the BOP contracts for in privately operated prisons, Residential Reentry Centers (i.e., halfway houses), and state and local correctional facilities.

than 2% of federal inmates were housed in a contract facility. The number of federal inmates in contract facilities increased to nearly 11% in FY1990, approximately 14% in FY2000, and nearly 18% in FY2010.

Figure 1. Federal Prison Population, FY1980-FY2012

Number of inmates in thousands

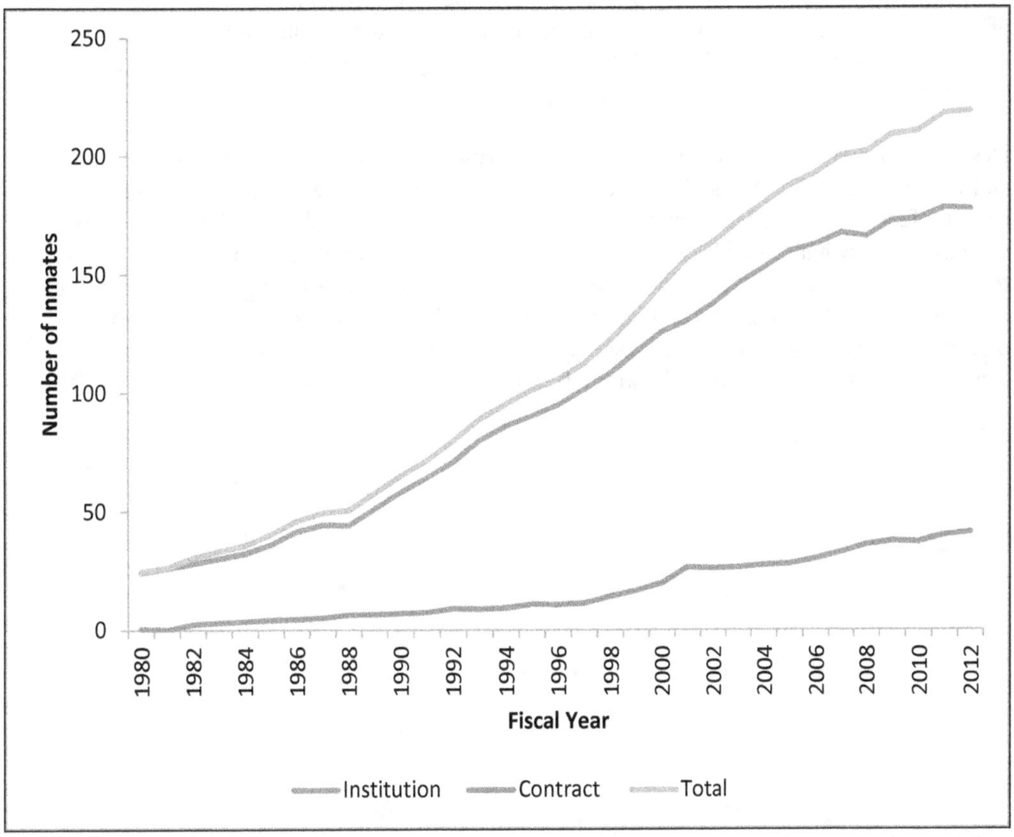

Source: Presentation of data provided by the U.S. Department of Justice, Bureau of Prisons.

The following discussion of some of the demographics of federal inmates uses data from the BJS rather than the BOP. BJS data on federal prisoners are only available for FY1998 through FY2010. Therefore, the BJS data cannot be used to show how these select demographics changed since the federal prison population started its sustained growth in the early 1980s. The proceeding discussion is intended to provide context for the discussion later in the report of potential policy options for addressing federal prison population growth.

Conviction Offense for Federal Inmates

As shown in **Figure 2**, in FY1998 approximately 18% of inmates entering the federal prison system were convicted for an immigration offense. There was a slight increase in the proportion of such inmates being sent to federal prison in both FY1999 and FY2000, but this trend was reversed by FY2002. However, in FY2003, the proportion of inmates entering the federal prison system for immigration offenses started an unabated increase. By FY2010, immigration offenders accounted for approximately 30% of all inmates entering the system that fiscal year. There was also a noticeable increase in the number of inmates entering the federal prison system for weapons-related convictions between FY1998 and FY2010, but it was not as pronounced as the increase in the number of inmates convicted for immigration offenses. Also, unlike the immigration offenders, the number of inmates entering federal prisons for weapons-related offenses has leveled-off. One other noticeable trend is the decrease in the number of inmates being sent to federal prison for violent and property crimes. In FY1998, violent and property offenders comprised approximately 9% and 18%, respectively, of all inmates entering federal prison. By FY2010, these offenders accounted for approximately 4% and 11% of prison admissions. The proportion of offenders entering federal prison for public order offenses[9] remained relatively consistent between FY1998 and FY2010.

Despite the increase in the number of inmates entering the federal prison system for immigration and weapons-related offenses, drug offenders still constitute the largest portion of inmates entering federal prisons. The number of inmates being sent to federal prison for drug offenses has decreased somewhat since FY1998 (when 41% of inmates entering federal prison were convicted for drug offenses). In every fiscal year between FY1998 and FY2010, drug offenders constituted the largest proportion of prison admissions, though in FY2009 and FY2010, immigration offenders were a close second. The vast majority of sentenced drug offenders, more than 95%,[10] were sent to federal prison for trafficking offenses.[11]

---

[9] Public order offenses include tax law violations; bribery; perjury; national defense; escape; racketeering and extortion; gambling; liquor; mailing or transporting of obscene materials; traffic; migratory birds; conspiracy, aiding and abetting, and jurisdictional offenses; violations of regulatory laws and regulations in agriculture, antitrust, labor law, food and drug, motor carrier, and other regulatory offenses.

[10] Data downloaded from U.S. Department of Justice, Office of Justice Programs, Bureau of Justice Statistics, *Federal Criminal Case Processing Statistics*, http://bjs.ojp.usdoj.gov/fjsrc/index.cfm.

[11] "Trafficking offenses" include an offense where an offender knowingly and intentionally imported or exported any controlled substance in schedule I, II, III, IV, or V (as defined by 21 U.S.C. §812). It includes manufacturing, distributing, dispensing, selling, or possessing with intent to manufacture, distribute, or sell a controlled substance or a counterfeit substance; exporting any controlled substance in schedules I-V; manufacturing or distributing a controlled substance in schedule I or II for purposes of unlawful importation; or making or distributing any punch, die, plate, stone, or any other thing designed to reproduce the label upon any drug or container, or removing or obliterating the label or symbol of any drug or container. It also includes knowingly opening, maintaining or managing any place for the purpose of manufacturing, distributing, or using any controlled substance (for example, 19 U.S.C. §1590; 21 U.S.C. §§333(e), 825(a)-(d), 830(a), 841(a)-(b) (d)(e)(g), 842(a), 843(a)(b), 845, 846, 848, 854, 856, 858, 859(a)(b), 860(a), 861(c)(f), 952(a)(b), 953(a)(e), 957, 959, 960(a)(b)(d), 961, 962, and 963; and 46A U.S.C. §§1903(g) and (j)). U.S. Department of Justice, Office of Justice Programs, Bureau of Justice Statistics, *Compendium of Federal Justice Statistics, 2004*, NCJ 213476, Washington, DC, December 2006, p. 119, http://www.bjs.gov/content/pub/pdf/cfjs04.pdf.

Figure 2. Conviction Offenses of Inmates Entering Federal Prison, FY1998-FY2010

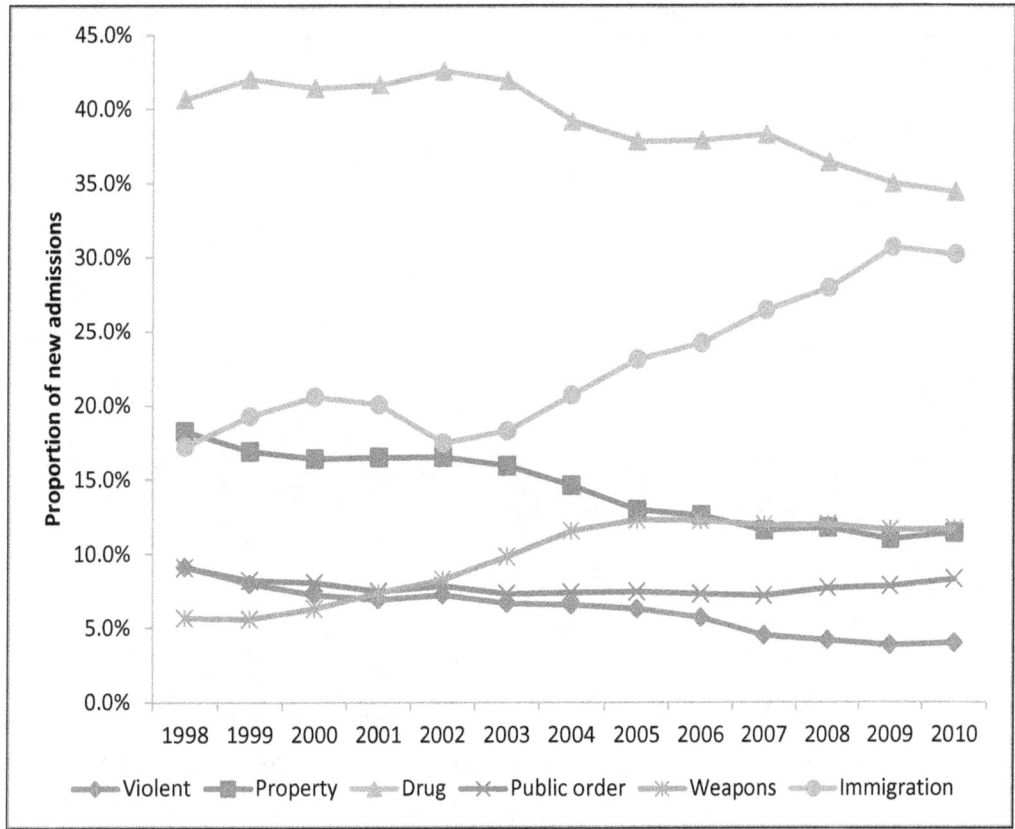

Source: Presentation of data from the U.S. Department of Justice, Bureau of Justice Statistics, Federal Criminal Case Processing Statistics.

Notes: Percentages were calculated excluding offenders whose conviction offense was classified as "unknown."

As shown in **Figure 3**, in FY1998, weapons and immigration offenders were 8.3% and 7.1%, respectively, of all federal inmates. By FY2010, weapons and immigration offenders comprised 15.5% and 11.6% of all federal inmates. By FY2010, approximately 8 out of every 10 inmates in federal prison were incarcerated for a drug, weapons, or immigration offense. While a growing proportion of federal inmates were incarcerated for drug, weapons, or immigration offenses, fewer inmates were incarcerated for violent offenses. In FY1998, nearly 12% of federal inmates were incarcerated for a violent offense; by FY2010, the proportion of federal inmates incarcerated for violent offenses decreased to 6.4%.

Figure 3. Inmates in Federal Prison at the End of the Fiscal Year, by Major Offense Type, FY1998-FY2010

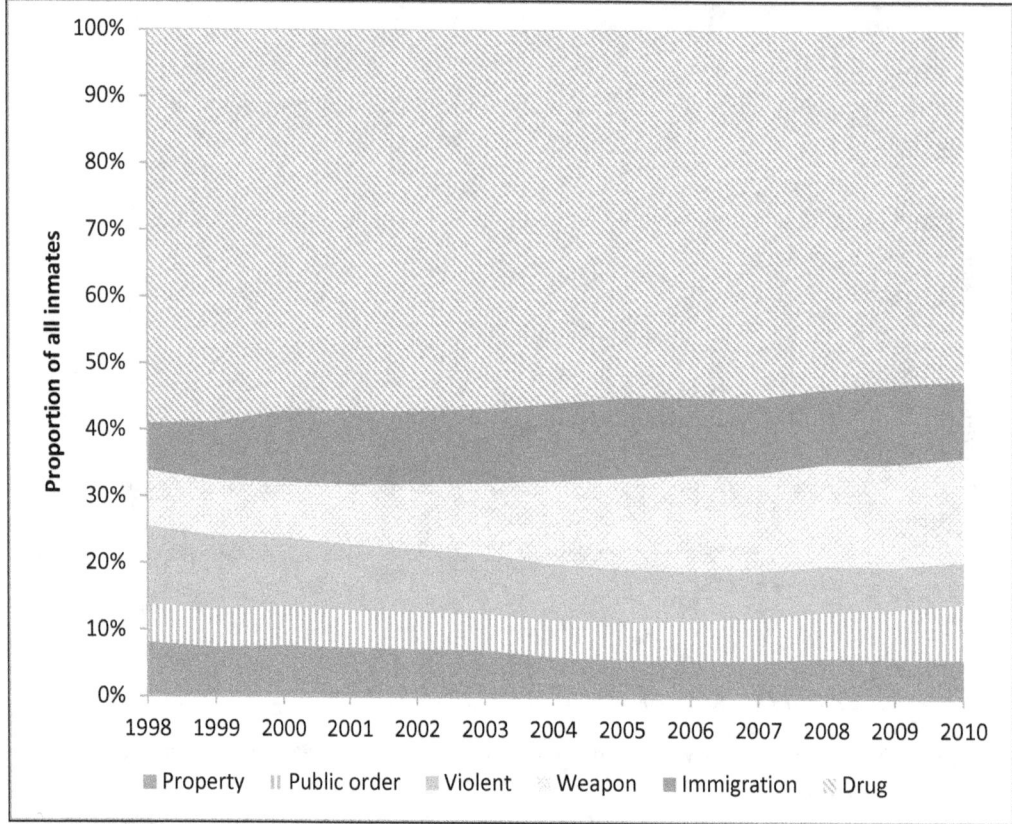

Source: Presentation of data from the U.S. Department of Justice, Bureau of Justice Statistics, Federal Criminal Case Processing Statistics.

Notes: Percentages were calculated excluding offenders whose sentence was classified as "unknown."

Length of Sentences for Federal Offenders

As shown in **Figure 4**, in any given fiscal year between FY1998 and FY2010, more than 7 in 10 inmates entering the federal prison system were sentenced to a term of incarceration that was five years or less. The data indicate two distinct trends in the sentencing of federal inmates. First, since FY1998 approximately three of every 10 inmates entering federal prisons were sentenced to a term of incarceration that was less than one year, though fewer inmates entered the federal prison system in FY2010 with a sentence of one year or less compared to FY1998. Second, since FY1998 there has been a slow, but steady, growth in the proportion of inmates sentenced to between three and five years of incarceration, and to a lesser extent, the proportion of inmates sentenced to between five and 10 years of incarceration.

Figure 4. Length of Sentence for Inmates Entering Federal Prison, FY1998-FY2010

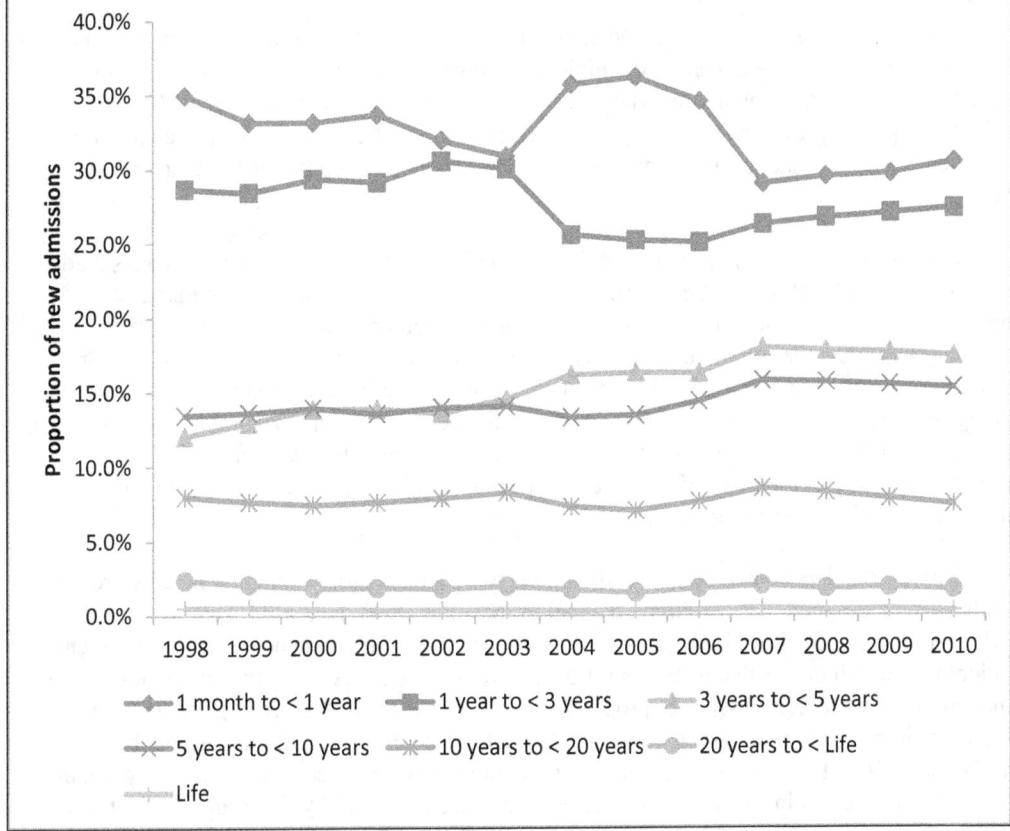

Source: Presentation of data from the U.S. Department of Justice, Bureau of Justice Statistics, Federal Criminal Case Processing Statistics.

Notes: Percentages were calculated excluding offenders whose sentence was classified as "unknown."

Policy Changes that Contributed to Prison Population Growth

A confluence of changes to federal sentencing and correctional policy since the early 1980s—including the expanded use of mandatory minimum penalties, the federalization of crime, and the abolition of parole for federal inmates—have contributed to the growing federal prison population. The expanded use of mandatory minimum penalties has resulted in offenders being sentenced to longer terms of imprisonment than they were 20 years ago. At the same time, the expanding federal criminal code, combined with greater enforcement of federal criminal statutes, has resulted in more people entering the federal criminal justice system. Thus, while more offenders are being arrested by federal law enforcement, tried in federal courts, and sentenced to incarceration in federal prisons for increasingly longer periods of time, the abolition of parole ensures that most inmates will serve all or nearly all of their sentences.

Mandatory Minimum Sentences

In a recent report, the United States Sentencing Commission (USSC) found that the enactment of a greater number of federal mandatory minimum sentences has, in part, contributed to the growing federal prison population. Mandatory minimum penalties have contributed to federal prison population growth because they have increased in number, have been applied to more offenses, required longer terms of imprisonment, and are used more frequently than they were 20 years ago.[12]

The number of mandatory minimum penalties in the federal code expanded as Congress made more offenses subject to such penalties. The USSC reported that the number of mandatory minimum penalties in the federal criminal code nearly doubled from 98 in 1991 to 195 in 2011.[13] Not only has there been an increase in the number of federal offenses that carry a mandatory minimum penalty, but offenders who are convicted of offenses with mandatory minimums are being sent to prison for longer periods. For example, the USSC found that, compared to FY1990 (43.6%), a larger proportion of defendants convicted of offenses that carried a mandatory minimum penalty in FY2010 (55.5%) were convicted of offenses that carried a mandatory minimum penalty of five years or more.[14]

While only offenders convicted for an offense carrying a mandatory minimum penalty are subject to those penalties, mandatory minimum penalties have, in effect, increased sentences for other offenders.[15] The USSC has incorporated many mandatory minimum penalties into the sentencing guidelines, which means that penalties for other offense categories under the guidelines had to increase in order to keep a sense of proportionality.[16] Research by the Urban Institute found that increases in expected time served contributed to half of the prison population growth between 1998 and 2010.[17] The increase in amount of time inmates were expected to serve was probably partially the result of inmates receiving longer sentences and partially the result of inmates being required to serve approximately 85% of their sentences after Congress eliminated parole for federal prisoners (this is discussed in greater detail in the "Eliminating Parole for Federal Inmates" section).

However, the increase in the federal prison population is not solely attributable to the increased use of mandatory minimum penalties. The USSC reported that the number of inmates in the

---

[12] U.S. Sentencing Commission, *Report to Congress: Mandatory Minimum Penalties in the Federal Criminal Justice System*, Washington, DC, October 2011, p. 63, http://www.ussc.gov/Legislative_and_Public_Affairs/ Congressional_Testimony_and_Reports/Mandatory_Minimum_Penalties/20111031_RtC_Mandatory_Minimum.cfm, hereinafter "*Mandatory Minimum Penalties in the Federal Criminal Justice System.*"

[13] Ibid., pp. 71-72.

[14] Ibid., p. 76.

[15] Erik Luna and Paul G. Cassell, "Mandatory Minimalism," *Cardozo Law Review*, vol. 32, no. 1 (September 2010), pp. 16-17; James E. Felman, on behalf of the American Bar Association, statement before the United States Sentencing Commission in the Hearing on Mandatory Minimums, May 27, 2010, p. 9, http://www.ussc.gov/ Legislative_and_Public_Affairs/Public_Hearings_and_Meetings/20100527/Testimony_Felman_ABA.pdf, hereinafter "Felman testimony."

[16] Ibid.

[17] Kamala Mallik-Kane, Barbara Parthasarathy, and William Adams, *Examining Growth in the Federal Prison Population, 1998 to 2010*, The Urban Institute, Washington, DC, September 2012, p. 10, http://www.urban.org/ UploadedPDF/412720-Examining-Growth-in-the-Federal-Prison-Population.pdf, hereinafter "*Examining Growth in the Federal Prison Population.*"

---

federal prison system who were convicted of an offense that carried a mandatory minimum penalty increased 178%, from approximately 40,000 in FY1995 to nearly 112,000 in FY2010.[18] Of these offenders, nearly 30,000 in FY1995 and approximately 80,000 in FY2010 were actually subject to a mandatory minimum penalty.[19] However, over the same time period there was a similar rate of growth in the number of inmates in federal prison who were not convicted of an offense that carried a mandatory minimum. In FY1995, nearly 32,000 inmates in federal prison were convicted of an offense that did not carry a mandatory minimum.[20] This increased 152%, to approximately 80,000 inmates, by FY2010.

Federalization of Crime

While the increase in the number of federal criminal statutes carrying a mandatory minimum sentence has contributed to the escalating federal prison population, the USSC also identified the federalization of crime[21] as another contributing factor to prison population growth. Over the past four decades the federalization of crime resulted in more people entering the federal criminal justice system as federal law enforcement agencies and the U.S. Attorneys Office started to enforce a broader array of federal offenses. The Urban Institute concluded that increased federal law enforcement activity contributed to about 13% of the growth in the federal prison population between 1998 and 2010, though the effects were not consistent across offense types and time.[22] For example, heightened immigration enforcement and increased investigation of weapons offenses contributed to approximately one-tenth of the population growth, but the growth in the prison population resulting from investigating more weapons offenses mainly occurred between 1998 and 2005.[23] However, decreased drug investigations reduced the federal prison population from what it might have been assuming that federal law enforcement priorities and practices had remained as they were in 1998.[24]

---

[18] The USSC limited its analysis of the number of inmates in federal prisons who were convicted of or subject to a mandatory minimum penalty to FY1995-FY2010 because the commission's analysis relied on combining USSC data with BOP data and there were limitations with the data prior to FY1995. *Mandatory Minimum Penalties in the Federal Criminal Justice System*, p. 81.

[19] Even though a defendant might be convicted for an offense that carries a mandatory minimum penalty there are mechanisms whereby the court may impose a term of imprisonment that is below the mandatory minimum (i.e., the defendant can be convicted for an offense carrying a mandatory minimum penalty, but the defendant is not subject to a mandatory minimum penalty when sentenced). For example, under 18 U.S.C. §3553(e), the court "[u]pon motion of the Government…shall have the authority to impose a sentence below a level established by statute as a minimum sentence so as to reflect a defendant's substantial assistance in the investigation or prosecution of another person who has committed an offense." Section 3553(e) also requires the sentence to be imposed in accordance with the federal sentencing guidelines.

[20] *Mandatory Minimum Penalties in the Federal Criminal Justice System*, p. 82.

[21] The USSC defined "federalization of crime" as the transformation of traditional state and local criminal offenses into federal crimes. Ibid., p. 63.

[22] *Examining Growth in the Federal Prison Population*, p. 10.

[23] Ibid.

[24] Ibid., p. 11.

Eliminating Parole for Federal Inmates

The BOP has identified the abolition of parole for federal inmates as one cause of the growing federal prison population.[25] The Comprehensive Crime Control Act of 1984 (P.L. 98-473) abolished parole for federal inmates and modified how much good time credit an inmate could earn. Anyone sentenced to incarceration for a federal crime committed after November 1, 1987, is not eligible for parole. Abolishing parole in the federal correctional system means that the BOP has not only had to confine a growing number of inmates, but it also has to confine them until they serve all, or nearly all, of their sentences. The BOP reported that as of September 30, 2012, only about 3% of inmates in federal prisons were still eligible to be paroled.[26] The remainder of federal inmates will have to serve their entire sentence, minus any good time credit they might earn.[27]

Issues Related to Prison Population Growth

The growth of the federal prison population has given rise to several issues of interest to policymakers. These include

- the increasing cost of operating the federal prison system;

- overcrowding in federal prisons;

- an increasing inmate-to-staff ratio; and

- a growing need for capital investment in correctional facilities.

Analysis of these issues is provided below.

Cost of Operating the Federal Prison System

The burgeoning prison population has contributed to mounting operational expenditures for the federal prison system. Congress funds BOP's operations through two accounts: Salaries and Expenses (S&E) and Buildings and Facilities (B&F).[28] The S&E account (i.e., the operating budget) provides for the custody and care of federal inmates and for the daily maintenance and operations of correctional facilities, regional offices, and BOP's central office in Washington, DC. It also provides funding for the incarceration of federal inmates in state, local, and private facilities. The B&F account (i.e., the capital budget) provides funding for the construction of new facilities and the modernization, repair, and expansion of existing facilities.

---

[25] U.S. Department of Justice, Bureau of Prisons, *A Brief History of the Bureau of Prisons*, http://www.bop.gov/about/history.jsp.

[26] Data provided by the U.S. Department of Justice, Bureau of Prisons.

[27] Each prisoner serving a term of imprisonment of more than one year, but not prisoners serving a life sentence, can receive a good time credit of up to 54 days per year to count toward serving the sentence. The amount of the credit is subject to the determination of the BOP. 18 U.S.C. §3624(b).

[28] For a more in-depth analysis of the BOP's appropriations, see CRS Report R42486, *The Bureau of Prisons (BOP): Operations and Budget*, by Nathan James.

As shown in **Figure 5**, the BOP's appropriations increased more than $6 billion from FY1980 ($330 million) to FY2012 ($6.641 billion). Between FY1980 and FY2012, the average annual increase in the BOP's appropriation was approximately $197 million. The data show that, by and large, growth in the BOP's appropriation is the result of ever-growing appropriations for the S&E account. This is not surprising considering the constant growth in the federal prison population and the fact that the S&E account provides funding for the care of federal inmates. Also, it has been argued that even though appropriations for the BOP's S&E account are discretionary, they are effectively mandatory because "[b]y law, the BOP must accept and provide for all [f]ederal inmates, including but not limited to inmate care, custodial staff, contract beds, food, and medical costs. The BOP cannot control the number of inmates sentenced to prison, and unlike other [f]ederal agencies, cannot limit assigned workloads and thereby control operating costs."[29] Appropriations for the B&F account have not grown as steadily as appropriations for the S&E account. This is, in part, explained by how funding for the B&F account is used; namely, Congress typically provides marked increases in this account only when there is a decision to expand prison capacity. For example, the noticeable spike in appropriations for the B&F account in FY1990 paved the way for an increase in BOP's prison capacity in the mid- to late 1990s.

---

[29] U.S. Congress, Senate Committee on Appropriations, Subcommittee on Commerce, Justice, Science, and Related Agencies, *Departments of Commerce and Justice, and Science, and Related Agencies Appropriations Bill, 2013*, report to accompany S. 2323, 112th Cong., 2nd sess., April 19, 2012, S.Rept. 112-158 (Washington: GPO, 2012), p. 64.

Figure 5. Appropriations for the BOP, FY1980-FY2012

Appropriations in billions of dollars

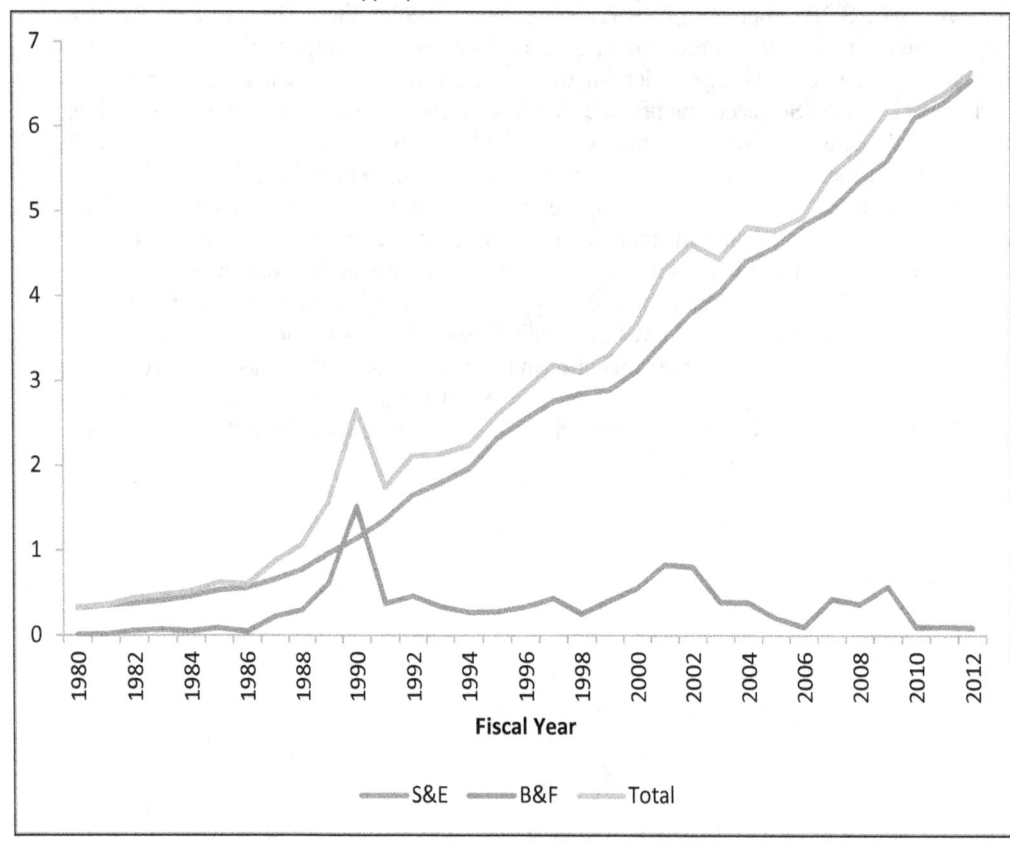

Source: Presentation of data provided by the U.S. Department of Justice, Bureau of Prisons.

Notes: Between FY1980 and FY1995, appropriations for the National Institute of Corrections (NIC) were provided in a separate account. After FY1995, the operating expenses for NIC are paid out of the BOP's S&E account. Therefore, to make appropriations for the S&E account as comparable as possible, appropriations for the NIC for FY1980-FY1995 were added to appropriations for the S&E account. Between FY1996 and FY2000, the BOP received an amount from the Violent Crime Reduction Trust Fund, which, according to the BOP, was used for substance abuse treatment. As such, these amounts were also added to the S&E account Appropriations include all supplemental and reprogrammed appropriations and rescissions to current year budget authority.

The BOP's expanding budget is starting to consume a larger share of the DOJ's overall annual appropriation. **Figure 6** shows what proportion of the DOJ's discretionary appropriation was for the BOP's overall appropriation and for the BOP's S&E appropriation, which has grown steadily along with the prison population. The BOP's overall budget is more susceptible to changes in year-to-year appropriations for the B&F account. The trend lines show that since FY1980 both the BOP's total budget and appropriations for the BOP's S&E account have, in general, encompassed a growing share of the DOJ annual appropriation. The noticeable spike in the BOP's share of the DOJ's annual appropriation in FY1990 was the result of Congress appropriating more than $1 billion for the B&F account. In addition, the decrease in the BOP's share of DOJ's appropriation observed in FY2009, a break in a general upward trend that started in FY2000, was the result of Congress appropriating an additional $4 billion for DOJ under the American Recovery and Reinvestment Act of 2009 (P.L. 111-5).

Figure 6. The BOP's Appropriation as a Share of the DOJ's Discretionary Budget Authority, FY1980-FY2012

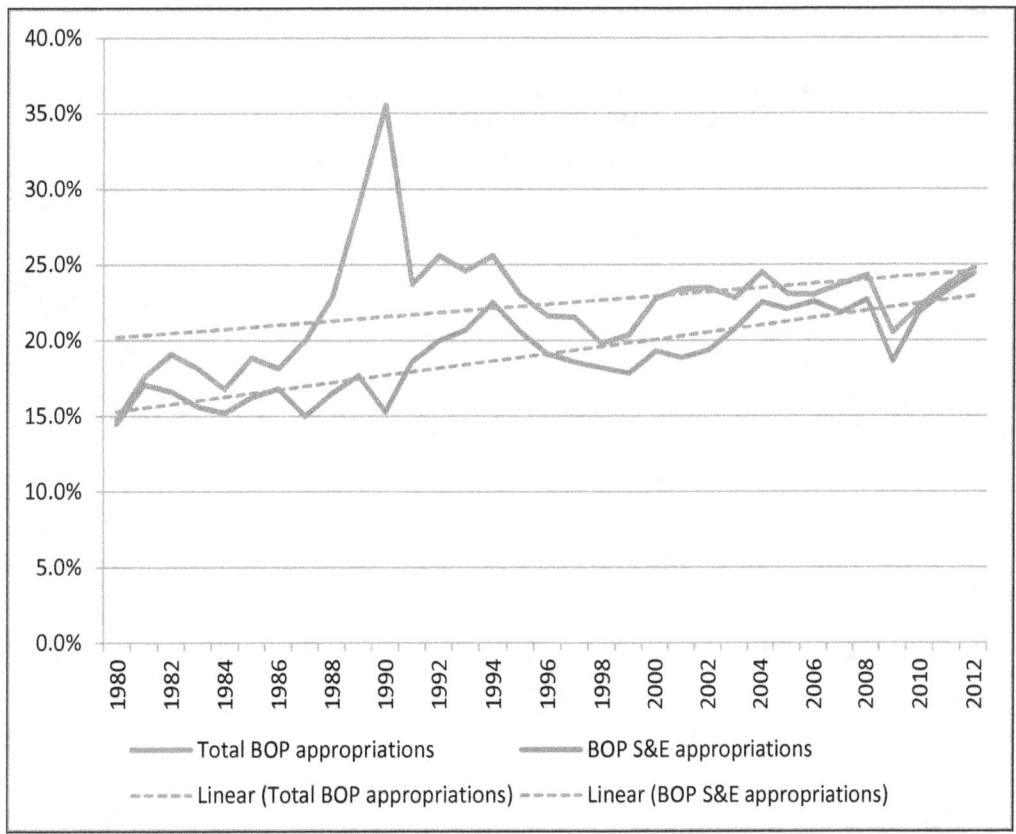

Source: The BOP's annual appropriation data was provided by the U.S. Department of Justice, Bureau of Prisons. Annual discretionary budget authority data for the Department of Justice were taken from Table 5.4 from the FY2013 *Budget of the United States Government.*

A comparison of the BOP's annual appropriations for its S&E and B&F accounts to the Administration's request for both accounts shows that Congress has been more likely to fund the Administration's request for prison construction and less likely to fully fund the Administration's request for the upkeep and care of the prison population. The requested appropriation indicates what the BOP believed it would need to properly manage the growing prison population each fiscal year. The data suggest that in many fiscal years the BOP operated with a budget below what it felt was adequate given the growing number of inmates under its jurisdiction.

The data presented in **Figure 7** show that between FY1980 and FY2012, Congress appropriated less than the Administration's request for the B&F account 14 times. Over the same time period Congress appropriated less than the Administration's request for the S&E account 20 times. In contrast to this general trend, however, the amount appropriated for the S&E account between FY2007 and FY2010 actually exceeded the Administration's request. The additional amounts, as noted by the House Committee on Appropriations, were to compensate for underfunding the BOP, which resulted in inadequate staffing levels and shortfalls in inmate programs.[30] Both the House

---

[30] U.S. Congress, House Committee on Appropriations, *Omnibus Appropriations Act, 2009*, committee print, 111th Cong., 1st sess., March 2009 (Washington: GPO, 2009), p. 274.

and Senate Committee on Appropriations reported that they felt that the Administration's requests for the BOP were inadequate for several years, which did not allow the bureau to meet its basic operational needs.[31]

Figure 7. Difference Between Appropriations and the Administration's Request for the BOP's S&E and B&F Accounts

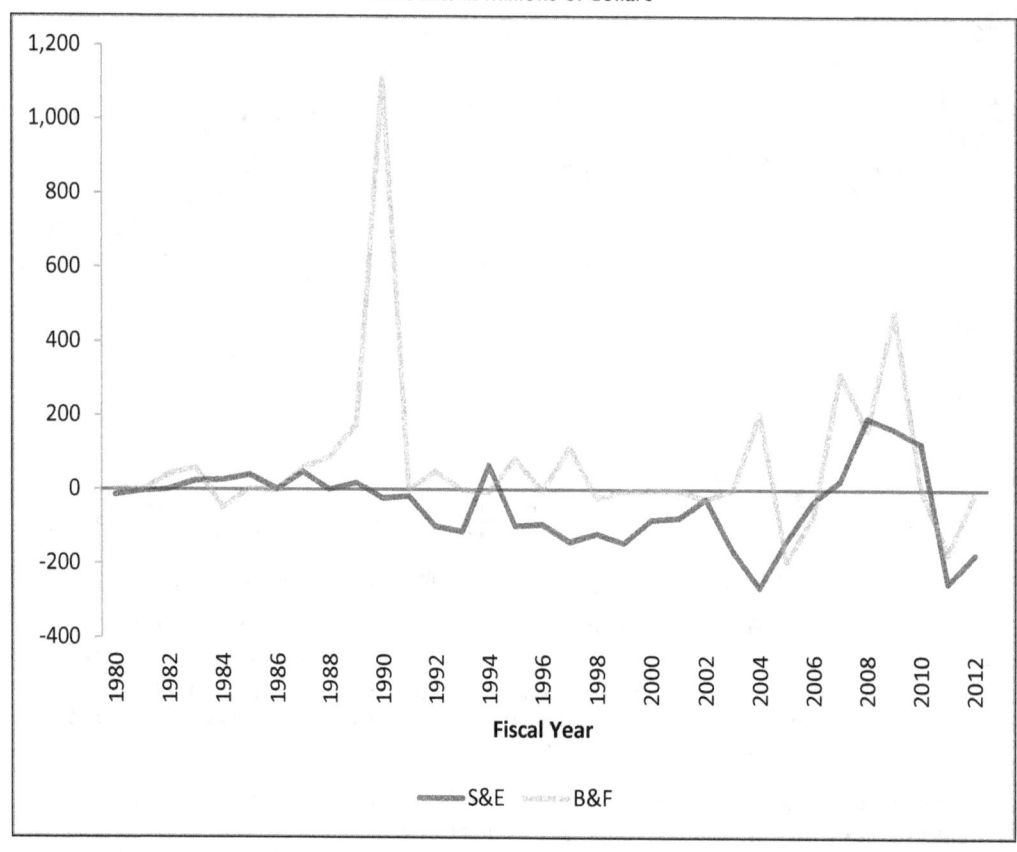

Amounts in millions of dollars

Source: Appropriated amounts were provided by the U.S. Department of Justice, Bureau of Prisons. The Administration's requested amounts were taken from the appendix to the *Budget of the United States Government*, for FY1980-FY2012.

Notes: Between FY1980 and FY1995, appropriations for the National Institute of Corrections (NIC) were provided in a separate account. After FY1995, the operating expenses for NIC are paid out of the BOP's S&E account. Therefore, to make appropriations for the S&E account as comparable as possible, appropriations for the NIC for FY1980-FY1995 were added to appropriations for the S&E account. Between FY1996 and FY2000, the BOP received an amount from the Violent Crime Reduction Trust Fund, which, according to the BOP, was used for substance abuse treatment. As such, these amounts were also added to the S&E account.

---

[31] Ibid. See also, U.S. Congress, House Committee on Appropriations, *Departments of Transportation and Housing and Urban Development, and Related Agencies Appropriations Act, 2010*, Conference Report to Accompany H.R. 3288, 111th Cong., 1st sess., December 8, 2009, H.Rept. 111-366 (Washington: GPO, 2009), p. 671; U.S. Congress, Senate Committee on Appropriations, Subcommittee on Commerce, Justice, Science, and Related Agencies, *Departments of Commerce and Justice, and Science, and Related Agencies Appropriations Bill, 2013*, report to accompany S. 2323, 112th Cong., 2nd sess., April 19, 2012, S.Rept. 112-158 (Washington: GPO, 2012), p. 65.

While it is not surprising that the BOP's annual appropriations would increase along with the prison population—after all, more inmates require more care and supervision, which requires additional funding—recent per capita expenditure data from the BOP indicate that it is getting more expensive each year to incarcerate an inmate in the federal system. As shown in **Table 1**, the overall per capita cost of incarcerating an inmate in the federal system has steadily increased from FY2000 to FY2012. Over this time period, the cost of incarceration rose from approximately $22,000 per inmate to more than $29,000 per inmate, an increase of 34.4%.

Table 1. Per Capita Cost of Incarceration in the Federal Prison System, FY2000-FY2012

| Fiscal Year | All of BOP | Security Level | | | | Federal Correctional Complexes[a] |
		High	Medium	Low	Minimum	
2000	$21,603	$26,518	$21,417	$18,407	$17,452	$21,360
2001	22,175	26,135	21,806	18,846	17,788	20,543
2002	22,518	27,456	21,473	19,228	18,770	21,538
2003	23,180	26,461	21,946	19,480	18,136	21,948
2004	23,267	26,951	21,896	19,242	17,647	21,764
2005	23,431	26,377	21,718	19,193	17,478	22,458
2006	24,439	25,398	23,648	20,834	17,291	23,152
2007	24,923	26,109	23,492	21,922	17,812	22,804
2008	25,895	27,924	24,065	23,373	19,635	23,958
2009	27,251	32,119	25,442	24,087	20,772	25,750
2010	28,282	33,858	26,248	25,377	21,005	27,267
2011	28,894	34,629	26,852	26,853	21,286	27,516
2012	29,027	34,046	26,686	27,166	21,694	27,683

Source: U.S. Department of Justice, Bureau of Prisons.

Notes: Per capita costs include support costs. The per capita cost of incarceration for all of BOP includes direct costs for federal detention centers, administrative security facilities, medical referral centers, privately operated institutions, residential reentry centers, and contracts with state and local institutions. It also includes support costs for federal detention centers, administrative security facilities, and medical referral centers.

a. Federal correctional complexes (FCC) contain two or more facilities with different security levels on the same grounds. For example, FCC Allenwood (PA) contains a high, medium, and low security facility.

However, the per capita cost of incarceration decreases as inmates are moved into lower-security level institutions. For example, in FY2012 it cost the BOP approximately $34,000 to house an inmate in a high-security facility. In comparison, it cost the BOP approximately $27,000 to house an inmate in either a medium- or low-security facility and nearly $22,000 to house an inmate in a minimum-security facility. This is partly because lower-security facilities do not require as many correctional officers; hence their operating expenditures are lower. In addition, the rated capacity for a facility decreases as the security level increases, meaning that higher-security facilities hold fewer inmates, which results in a higher per capita cost of incarceration for higher-security facilities. For example, even if the total operating expenditures for a high- and a low-security facility were the same for any given fiscal year, the per capita expenditure in the high-security facility would be greater because it held fewer inmates.

The BOP has identified rising utility, food, and medical care costs as three of the primary drivers of the increasing cost of the federal prison system.[32] The BOP's expenditures on utilities, food, and medical care have generally increased each fiscal year since FY2000.[33] Moreover, as shown in **Figure 8**, the per-inmate cost for utilities, food, and medical care has increased, although, the per capita increase in the cost of food and utilities has not been as pronounced as the increase in the per capita cost of inmate medical care. The medical costs for the BOP are most likely increasing as the result of the general upward climb of health care costs in the United States, with annual increases in health care costs outstripping inflation.[34] The BOP reported that an increasing number of federal inmates require medical care, primarily as a result of the expanding inmate population. According to the BOP, conditions such as diabetes, hypertension, and infectious diseases have a slightly higher rate of incidence in the incarcerated population.[35] In addition, the federal prison population is aging—BJS data shows that at the end of FY2010 approximately 14% of federal inmates were over the age of 50 and nearly 4% were over the age of 60—and in general, older individuals require more medical care.

---

[32] U.S. Department of Justice, Bureau of Prisons, FY2013 Performance Budget, Congressional Submission, Salaries and Expenses, pp. 22, 25, and 42, http://www.justice.gov/jmd/2013justification/pdf/fy13-bop-se-justification.pdf; hereinafter, BOP's FY2013 S&E Budget Justification.

[33] Data provided by the Bureau of Prisons.

[34] Alex Nussbaum, "Health Care Costs Rise Faster Than U.S. Inflation Rate," *Bloomberg*, May 21, 2012, http://www.bloomberg.com/news/2012-05-21/health-care-costs-rise-faster-than-u-s-inflation-rate.html.

[35] BOP's FY2013 S&E Budget Justification, p. 21.

Figure 8. Per Capita Cost ($) of Medical Care, Utilities, and Food, FY2000-FY2012

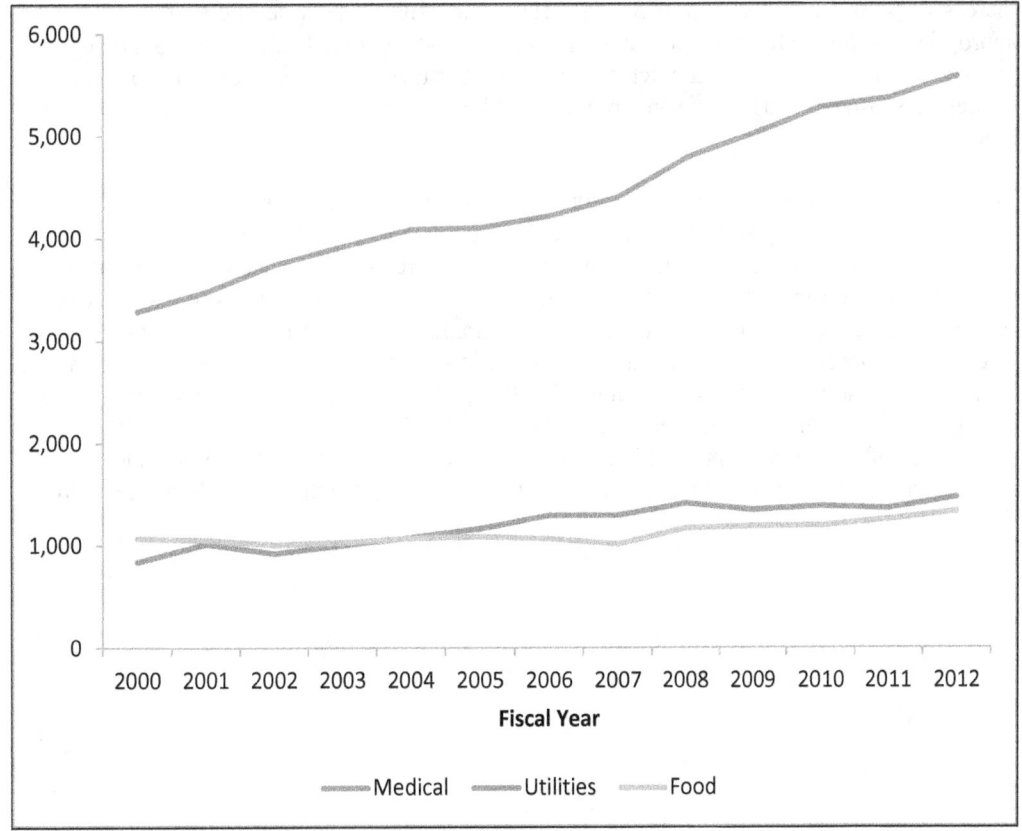

Source: Based on a CRS analysis of data provided by the U.S. Department of Justice, Bureau of Prisons.

Notes: Per capita costs were calculated using figures on the number of inmates held in BOP facilities at the end of the fiscal year.

In addition to the rising cost of utilities, food, and medical care, the cost of providing rehabilitative programs for inmates has generally increased since FY2000 (see **Figure 9**). On a per capita basis, the BOP spends the most on education programs for inmates. In FY2012, the BOP spent nearly $275 more per inmate for education programs than it did in FY2000. The BOP had similar per capita costs for substance abuse treatment programs and psychological services between FY2000 and FY2005. However, after FY2005, the per capita costs for substance abuse treatment started to grow at a rate that exceeded that of psychological services.

The growing cost of providing education and substance abuse treatment programs might be the result of the BOP's need to expand access to programming in order to meet increasing demand. Under current law, the BOP is required to provide a functional literacy program for all mentally capable inmates who are not functionally literate and to offer literacy/General Equivalency Diploma (GED) programs for inmates who have not earned a high school diploma or its equivalent.[36] In addition, federal inmates are required to make satisfactory progress toward earning a high school diploma or a GED in order to earn their full allotment of good time credit.[37]

---

[36] See 18 U.S.C. §3624(f)(1) and 18 U.S.C. §3624(b)(3).

[37] Each prisoner serving a term of imprisonment of more than one year, but not prisoners serving a life sentence, can (continued...)

The BOP reports that since these requirements went into effect, demand for literacy programs has increased.[38] Also, current law (18 U.S.C. §3621) requires BOP to provide, subject to appropriations, residential substance abuse treatment[39] and appropriate aftercare[40] for all eligible prisoners.[41] Prisoners who are convicted of nonviolent crimes and who successfully complete a residential substance abuse treatment program are eligible to have their sentence reduced by not more than one year.[42]

The BOP reports that in FY2007 and FY2008, it was not able to provide substance abuse treatment to all eligible prisoners due to inadequate funding for program expansion; but, after an investment in expanding drug treatment services, the BOP reports that since FY2009 it has been able to provide substance abuse treatment to all eligible inmates.[43] Obligations for psychology services include funding for most rehabilitative programming (e.g., mental health and sex offender treatment) other than education programs and substance abuse treatment. Per capita cost for psychology services increased starting in FY2007, which roughly coincides with provisions in the Adam Walsh Child Protection and Safety Act of 2006 (P.L. 109-248) requiring the BOP to provide sex offender treatment to all inmates who are in need of and suitable for it, and with the requirements in the Second Chance Act of 2007 (P.L. 110-199) that the BOP help prepare inmates for re-entry.

(...continued)

receive a good time credit of up to 54 days per year to count toward serving the sentence. The amount of the credit is subject to the determination of BOP. 18 U.S.C. §3624(b).

[38] BOP's FY2013 S&E Budget Justification, p. 26.

[39] "Residential substance abuse treatment" is defined as a course of individual and group activities and treatment, lasting at least six months, in residential treatment facilities set apart from the general prison population (which may include pharmacotherapies, where appropriate) that may extend beyond the six-month period. 18 U.S.C. §3621(e)(5)(A).

[40] "Aftercare" is defined as placement, case management, and monitoring in a community-based substance abuse treatment program when the prisoner leaves the custody of BOP. 18 U.S.C. §3621(e)(5)(C).

[41] An "eligible prisoner" is defined as a prisoner who is determined by BOP to have a substance abuse problem and to be willing to participate in a residential substance abuse treatment program. 18 U.S.C. §3621(e)(5)(B).

[42] The following categories of inmates are not eligible for early release: (1) Immigration and Customs Enforcement detainees; (2) pretrial inmates; (3) contractual boarders (for example, District of Columbia, state, or military inmates); (4) inmates who have a prior felony or misdemeanor conviction for homicide, forcible rape, robbery, or aggravated assault, or child sexual abuse offenses; (5) inmates who are not eligible for participation in a community-based program as determined by the institution's warden on the basis of his or her professional discretion; or (6) inmates whose current offense is a felony. 28 C.F.R. §550.55.

[43] BOP's FY2013 S&E Budget Justification, p. 27.

Figure 9. Per Capita Cost ($) of Rehabilitative Programs, FY2000-FY2012

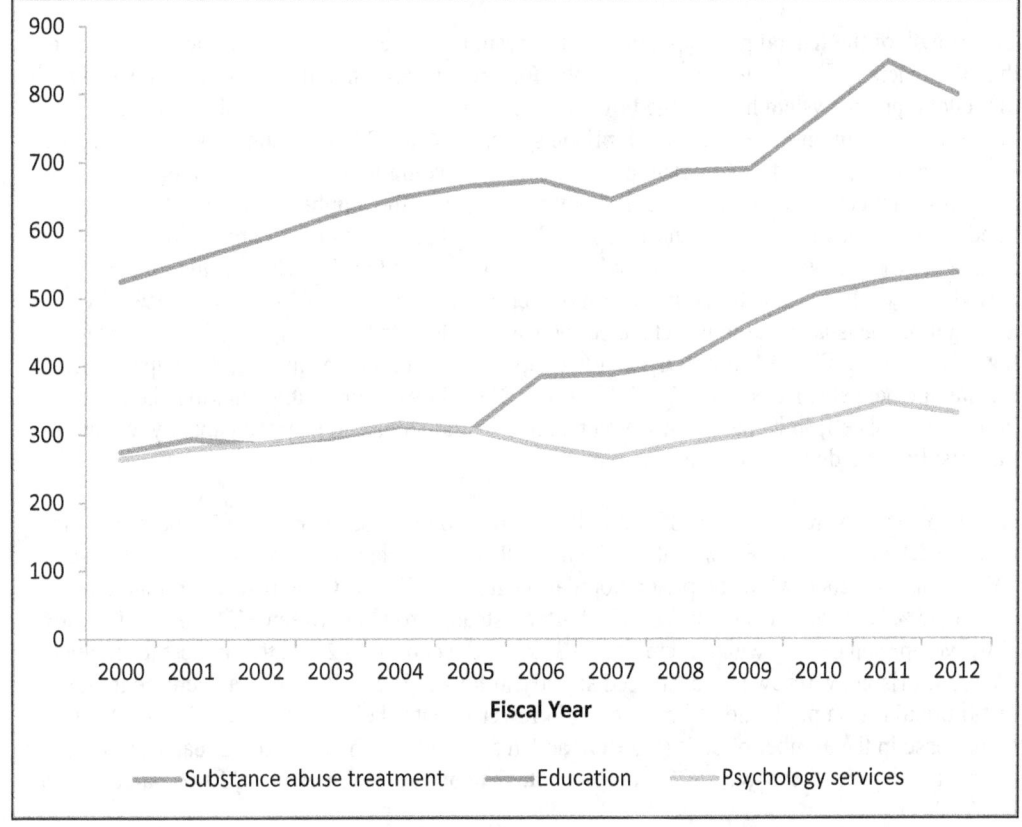

Source: Based on a CRS analysis of data provided by the U.S. Department of Justice, Bureau of Prisons.

Notes: Per capita costs were calculated using figures on the number of inmates held in BOP facilities at the end of the fiscal year.

The increasing cost of operating the federal prison system might be an issue for Congress as policymakers seek to find ways to reduce discretionary spending. The appropriations committees have already expressed concern that the continued growth in the federal prison population is not sustainable.[44] Unless there is a change in the upward trajectory in the number of inmates in the federal prison system, Congress will face a decision regarding appropriation of additional funds for the BOP. Assuming that growth in the budgetary requirements for the BOP exceeds the growth in the allocation for the Administration of Justice budget function under the annual budget resolution, policymakers might face a choice to reduce appropriations for other DOJ agencies or DOJ grant programs in order to fund the federal prison system.

---

[44] In the conference report for the Consolidated and Further Continuing Appropriations Act, 2012 (i.e., the "minibus," P.L. 112-55), the conferees expressed concern that "the current upward trend in the prison inmate population is unsustainable and, if left unchecked, will eventually engulf the [Department of Justice's] budgetary resources." U.S. Congress, House of Representatives, *Agriculture, Rural Development, Food and Drug Administration, and the Related Agencies Programs for the Fiscal Year Ending September 30, 2012, and for Other Purposes*, Conference Report to Accompany H.R. 2112, 112th Cong., 1st sess., November 14, 2011, H.Rept. 112-284 (Washington, DC: GPO, 2011), p. 241.

Prison Overcrowding

The growth of the federal prison population has resulted in the BOP incarcerating more inmates than the federal prison system is rated to hold. **Figure 10** shows that the level of overcrowding in the federal prison system has changed over the years. Overcrowding reflects the difference between how many inmates the federal prison system is "rated" to hold and how many inmates the system actually holds.[45] For example, if the overcrowding level is 35%, this means that the number of inmates held in the federal system is 35% above the number of inmates the system is rated to hold. Between FY1991 and FY1997, the federal prison system's capacity nearly doubled (a 95.2% increase) while the institutional population increased by 57.0% over this same time period. The BOP was able to reduce prison overcrowding between FY1991 and FY1997 by adding more bedspace, but it also changed the way it calculated rated capacity for each of its facilities. Prior to FY1991, the BOP calculated its capacity based on single cell occupancy (i.e., one inmate per cell). But starting in FY1991, the BOP allowed for double bunking (i.e., two inmates to one cell) in its facilities, which resulted in an increase in its rated capacity, which in turn resulted in a decrease in overcrowding.

Data show that overcrowding in BOP facilities started to increase after FY1997, and it peaked in FY2004 when overcrowding was at 41%. The BOP's prison capacity expanded 30.7% between FY1997 and FY2004 while the prison population grew by 50.9%. Overcrowding remained around 35% between FY2005 and FY2010 after a steady growth between FY1997 and FY2004. However, prison overcrowding increased to 39% by the end of FY2011, the highest level since FY2004. Prison overcrowding decreased slightly in FY2012 to 38%, due to a decrease in the institutional prison population (there were 378 fewer inmates held in BOP facilities in FY2012), an increase in the number of beds (the BOP added 567 beds in FY2012), and greater use of contract bedspace (there were 1,297 more inmates in contract facilities in FY2012 than there were in FY2011).

---

[45] Rated capacity, as calculated by the BOP, assumes some level of double bunking (i.e., two inmates to a cell) across the federal prison system. The amount of double bunking allowed depends on the facility's security level (i.e., minimum, low, medium, or high). The BOP calculates each facility's rated capacity using the following formulas: minimum and low security institutions at 100 percent double bunking; medium security institutions at 50 percent double bunking and; high security institutions at 25 percent double bunking. For example, if a high security facility had 500 cells, the facility's rated capacity would be 625 inmates. The rated capacity is intended to reflect the number of prisoners that the institution can house safely and securely with adequate access to services and rehabilitative programs.

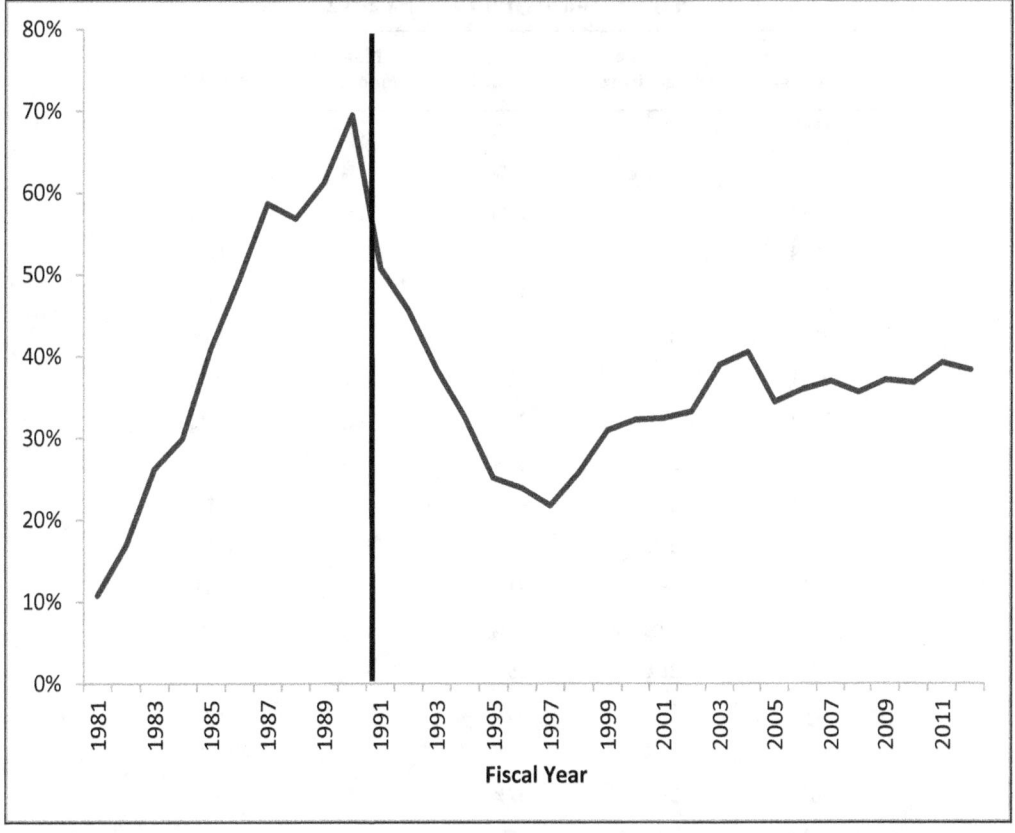

Figure 10. Overcrowding in the Federal Prison System, FY1981-FY2012

Source: FY1981-FY2012 crowding levels were provided by the U.S. Department of Justice, Bureau of Prisons.

Notes: Overcrowding rates for FY1981-FY1990 are not directly comparable to crowding rates after FY1990 because the BOP changed the way that it calculated its capacity.

Data from the BOP indicate that while federal prisons have been operating at 30% or more over rated capacity for more than a decade, the overcrowding problem is worse in high- and medium-security male facilities (see **Table 2**). Medium-security male facilities were operating at well over 50% of rated capacity for the early part of the previous decade. Overcrowding in medium-security facilities was brought down in the latter part of the previous decade because the BOP opened several additional facilities, but medium security overcrowding levels have been slowly increasing since FY2006. For the earlier part of the previous decade, overcrowding in high security male facilities, in general, was not as bad as it was in medium security facilities. However, since FY2006, high security facilities have been more crowded than medium and low security facilities and above the average overcrowding within the federal prison system in general. Since FY2006, overcrowding in high security male facilities has been near or above 50%.

Table 2. Overcrowding in All BOP facilities and Low-, Medium-, and High-Security Male Facilities, FY1995-FY2012

Fiscal Year	All Facilities	Male Low	Male Medium	Male High
1995	25%	33%	52%	40%
1996	24%	31%	42%	65%
1997	22%	23%	37%	52%
1998	26%	27%	48%	56%
1999	31%	37%	51%	51%
2000	32%	42%	50%	54%
2001	32%	38%	58%	42%
2002	33%	39%	58%	41%
2003	39%	39%	59%	58%
2004	41%	45%	62%	49%
2005	34%	43%	42%	35%
2006	36%	41%	37%	53%
2007	37%	35%	42%	53%
2008	36%	35%	44%	50%
2009	37%	40%	47%	49%
2010	37%	37%	43%	53%
2011	39%	37%	51%	55%
2012	38%	40%	47%	51%

Source: U.S. Department of Justice, Bureau of Prisons.

Notes: All BOP facilities include minimum security male facilities and secure female facilities, in addition to low, medium, and high security male facilities.

The BOP has attempted to address prison overcrowding by placing a growing proportion of federal inmates in contract facilities. While this has undoubtedly helped control prison overcrowding to some degree, it is also drawing resources away from BOP's other operations. **Figure 11** shows how growth in funding for the Contract Confinement[46] decision unit compares to growth in the Inmate Care and Programs[47] and Institutional Security and Administration[48]

---

[46] This decision unit provides for the costs associated with the confinement of federal inmates in contract facilities, which include private prisons, residential re-entry centers, state and local facilities, and home confinement. It provides funding for the management and oversight of contract confinement functions. The decision unit also provided funding for the National Institute of Corrections.

[47] This decision unit covers the cost of inmate food, medical supplies, institutional and release clothing, welfare services, transportation, gratuities, staff salaries, and operational costs of functions directly related to providing inmate care. It provides funding for inmate programs, including education and vocational training, psychological services, religious programs, and drug treatment. All of the drug treatment programs discussed above are funded from this decision unit. The decision unit also covers costs associated with regional and central office administration and support related to providing inmate care.

[48] This decision unit covers costs associated with the maintenance of facilities and institution security. It funds institution maintenance, motor pool operations, powerhouse operations, institution security and other administrative (continued...)

decision units and the S&E account overall. **Figure 11** shows that in most fiscal years since FY1999, growth in funding for contract confinement exceeded that of the S&E account overall. Increased funding for contract confinement has come at the cost of slower growth for the Inmate Care and Programs and Institutional Security and Administration decision units, especially the latter, which in most fiscal years grew at a rate below either the S&E account or the Inmate Care and Programs decision unit, or both.

Figure 11. Growth in Funding for Contract Confinement, Inmate Care and Programs, Institutional Security and Administration, and Overall Salaries and Expenses

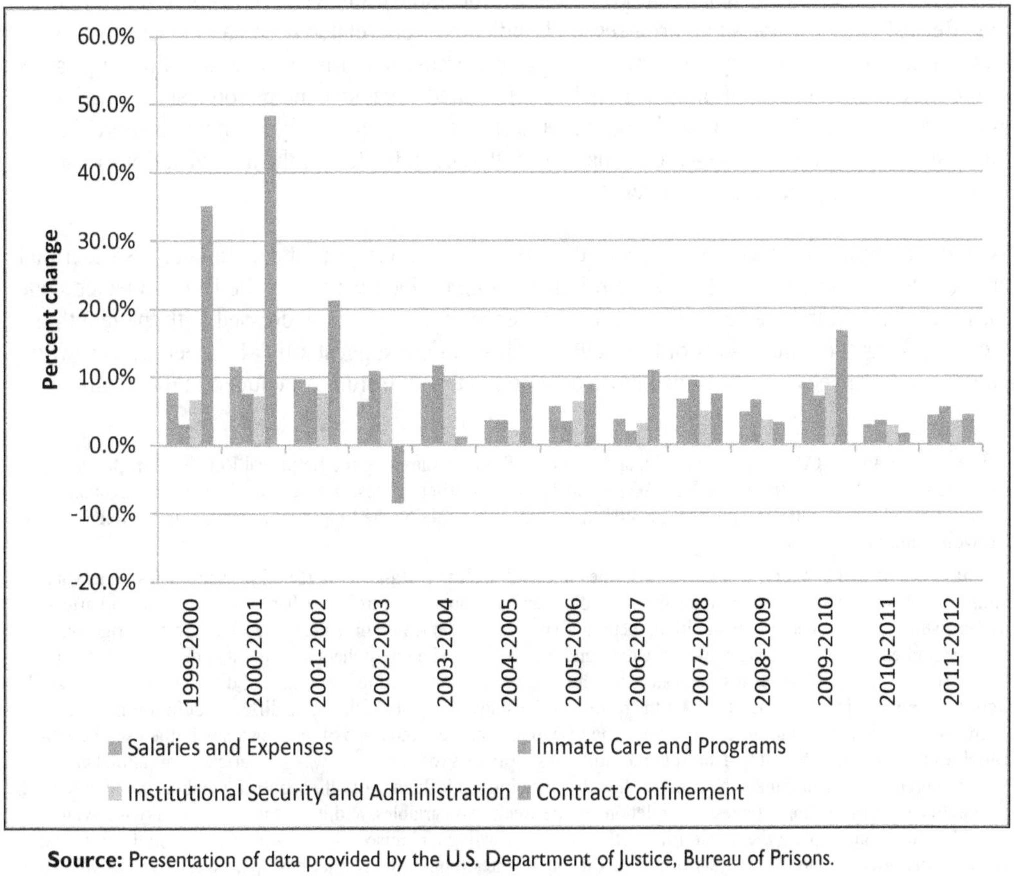

Source: Presentation of data provided by the U.S. Department of Justice, Bureau of Prisons.

Notes: Figure does not include funding for the Management and Administration decision unit.

Continued increases in prison overcrowding could be an issue for Congress given concerns about a potential link between prison overcrowding and increases in assaults and other inmate misconduct. Research on the link between prison overcrowding and inmate misconduct has been inconsistent, with some research showing a positive association between the two, other research

_____

(...continued)

functions. The decision unit also covers costs associated with regional and central office administrative and management support functions such as research and evaluation, systems support, financial management, budget functions, safety, and legal counsel.

showing no relationship, and some research even suggesting that there is a negative relationship between overcrowding and misconduct (i.e., as overcrowding increases, misconduct decreases).[49] A group of researchers conducted a meta-analysis that sought to synthesize the results of research on the overcrowding-misconduct link. Their research, which was based on 16 studies that provided 120 estimates of the correlation between overcrowding and inmate misconduct, concluded that, overall, overcrowding did not substantially influence inmate misconduct.[50]

Based on its own research, in which it collected data from 73 all-male low-, medium-, and high-security federal prisons from July 1996 to December 2004, the BOP concluded that there is a significant positive relationship between overcrowding and misconduct. The analysis conducted by the BOP included statistical methods to control for stable traits within each prison and to test the effect of other variables that prior research indicated were related to inmate misconduct. The BOP estimated that for every one percentage point increase in a prison's overcrowding (measured as the ratio of the number of inmates to the prison's rated capacity), the prison's annual serious assault rate increased by 4.1 assaults per 5,000 inmates.[51] To put this figure in perspective, in 2009 (the most recent year data are available), BOP data indicate that the annual serious assault rate was 16 assaults per 5,000 inmates.[52]

Why do the results of the BOP's analysis disagree with the results of the meta-analysis described above? One possible explanation is the relatively long period over which the BOP collected data for its study. Research has shown that the prevalence of misconduct increased with the length of the study.[53] As such, the results of the BOP's analysis might suggest a link between overcrowding and misconduct because it included more data points than the studies included in the meta-

---

[49] Travis W. Franklin, Courtney A. Franklin, and Travis C. Pratt, "Examining the Empirical Relationship Between Prison Crowding and Inmate Misconduct: A Meta-analysis of Conflicting Research Results," *Journal of Criminal Justice*, vol. 34, no. 4 (July-August 2006), p. 401, hereinafter "Examining the Empirical Relationship Between Prison Crowding and Inmate Misconduct."

[50] It has been argued that this body of research does not lend itself to meta-analytic techniques because studies vary in units of analysis, the definition of prison overcrowding, and attempts to control for other variables that could affect the overcrowding-misconduct link. In addition, meta-analytic techniques would give the same weight to both rigorous and cursory studies of the link between overcrowding and misconduct. The researchers incorporated these concerns into their research design. Their results suggested that the effect sizes calculated using studies of differing methodological rigor were not dissimilar enough to affect the results of the study. They also found that different definitions of prison overcrowding did not lead to different results. The researchers address the issue of inconsistency in the use of control variables across studies by using data from the study to simply test whether there was a bivariate correlation between prison overcrowding and inmate misconduct, thereby negating the influence of other control variables in the outcome. While this is the most simplistic test of a relationship between two variables, and it does not exclude any intervening variables that might explain the relationship between overcrowding and misconduct, it stands to reason that introducing any control variables into the analysis would only dissipate the strength of any relationship between overcrowding and misconduct. Because the researchers concluded that there is not a relationship to begin with, it appears unlikely that additional variables would change their conclusion. Ibid., pp. 407-408. Gerald G. Gaes, *Prison Crowding Research Reexamined*, U.S. Department of Justice, Bureau of Prisons, Washington, DC, January 1994, p. 65, http://www.bop.gov/news/research_projects/published_reports/cond_envir/oreprvariance.pdf.

[51] U.S. Department of Justice, Bureau of Prisons, *The Effects of Changing Crowding and Staffing Levels in Federal Prisons on Inmate Violence Rates, Executive Summary*, October 2005, hereinafter "*The Effects of Changing Crowding and Staffing Levels in Federal Prisons on Inmate Violence Rates.*"

[52] Based on data downloaded from U.S. Department of Justice, Bureau of Prisons, *Assault Graph Spreadsheets by Year*, http://www.bop.gov/news/research_projects/assaults/assault_spreadsheets/assaults_graph_spreadsheets_by_year.jsp. The annual assault rate was calculated using the total number of serious assaults against both inmates and correctional officers and the average annual prison population over each of the 12 months in the year.

[53] John Wooldredge, Timothy Griffin, and Travis Pratt, "Considering Hierarchical Models for Research on Inmate Behavior: Predicting Misconduct with Multilevel Data," *Justice Quarterly*, vol. 18, no. 1 (March 2001), p. 212.

---

analysis. Also, it has been argued that because of differences between federal and state prisons, the results of research that tests the link between overcrowding and misconduct in the federal prison system might not be directly comparable to similar analyses using state-level data.[54] If this is the case, the results of the meta-analysis may not be directly comparable to the results of the BOP's study because most of the studies included in the meta-analysis used state-level data.

A Government Accountability Office (GAO) report on prison crowding highlights some of the problems overcrowding can cause in BOP facilities and how those problems might contribute to inmate misconduct. The GAO reported that in order to manage the growing inmate population, the BOP has had to triple or quadruple bunk some inmates and in other instances the BOP has had to convert common areas, such as a television room, into temporary housing space, which can result in inmates with a higher propensity for violence spending more time with other inmates.[55] In addition, due to prison crowding, inmates may experience crowded bathroom facilities, reduced shower times, shortened meal times, longer waits for food service, and limited recreational activities.[56] The increasing number of inmates housed in BOP facilities might decrease the availability of program opportunities, resulting in inmate idleness and waiting lists for rehabilitative programs like education, vocation training, substance abuse treatment, and faith-based reentry programs.[57]

The reduction in rehabilitation opportunities can affect the BOP's ability to manage the prison population. As mentioned above, inmates who successfully complete a residential substance abuse treatment program can have up to one year taken off of their sentence. However, the BOP reported long wait lists for admission to a residential substance abuse treatment program, which limited the BOP's ability to admit inmates early enough to allow them to earn the maximum reduction in their sentences.[58] Also, under current law, in order for inmates to earn their full allotment of good time credit per year, one of the conditions is that the inmate is making satisfactory progress on completing a GED (assuming the inmate does not have a GED or a high school diploma).[59] Overcrowding can also decrease the number of meaningful work opportunities available to inmates. Within any given prison there are only so many jobs related to operating and maintaining the prison for inmates to participate in, and with recent changes to how executive branch agencies procure goods produced by the Federal Prison Industries (FPI), there are fewer opportunities for an inmate to work in a FPI factory.[60]

---

[54] Benjamin Steiner and John Wooldredge, "Rethinking the Link Between Institutional Crowding and Inmate Misconduct," *The Prison Journal*, vol. 89, no. 2 (June 2009), pp. 227-228.

[55] U.S. Government Accountability Office, *Bureau of Prisons: Growing Inmate Crowding Negatively Affects Inmates, Staff, and Infrastructure*, GAO-12-742, September 2012, p. 18, http://www.gao.gov/assets/650/648123.pdf, hereinafter "GAO prison crowding report."

[56] Ibid., p. 19.

[57] Ibid., pp. 19-20.

[58] Ibid., pp. 20-21.

[59] 18 U.S.C. §3624(b)(1).

[60] For more information on changes in how executive branch agencies procure goods produced by the FPI and the number of inmates working in FPI factories, see CRS Report RL32380, *Federal Prison Industries: Overview and Legislative History*, by Nathan James.

Inmate-to-Staff Ratio

Another issue related to the growth of the federal prison population is increasing inmate-to-staff ratios. **Table 3** shows both the inmate-to-staff ratio and the inmate-to-correctional officer ratio for the federal prison system since FY2000.[61] The inmate-to-staff ratio has held steady (approximately five inmates to every BOP staff member) since FY2005, but this is higher than the inmate-to-staff ratio in FY2000 (approximately four inmates to every BOP staff member). The inmate-to-correctional officer ratio has been approximately twice the inmate-to-staff ratio. The ratio of inmates to correctional officers was approximately 10 to 1 in FY2012, roughly the same as it was in FY2000. However, the inmate-to-correctional officer ratio was nearly 11 to 1 in FY2004 and FY2005. The inmate-to-correctional officer ratio has remained fairly steady even though the BOP has increased the number of correctional officers by 2% or more in 9 of the past 13 fiscal years. To put these figures in perspective, the Bureau of Justice Statistics reports that in 2005, the inmate-to-staff ratio for all state correctional agencies was 3.3 to 1 and the ratio of inmates to correctional officers was 4.9 to 1.[62] The inmate-to-staff and inmate-to-correctional officer ratios for the five largest state correctional systems (in terms of inmate population) in 2005 were, respectively,

- California: 3.6 to 1 and 6.1 to 1,

- Texas: 4.3 to 1 and 5.9 to 1,

- Florida: 3.8 to 1 and 4.9 to 1,

- New York: 2 to 1 and 3 to 1, and

- Georgia: 3.6 to 1 and 5.4 to 1.[63]

---

[61] "Staff" includes all employees of a facility whereas "correctional officers" only include employees whose primary duties are to supervise inmates.

[62] James J. Stephen, *Census of State and Federal Correctional Facilities, 2005*, U.S. Department of Justice, Office of Justice Programs, Bureau of Justice Statistics, NCJ 222182, Washington , DC, October 2008, p. 5, http://bjs.ojp.usdoj.gov/content/pub/pdf/csfcf05.pdf.

[63] Ibid., p. 22.

**Table 3. Inmate-to-Staff and Inmate-to-Correctional Officer Ratios
for the Federal Prison System**

	Number of Inmates per...	
Fiscal Year	All BOP Staff	Correctional Officers
2000	4.1	9.9
2001	4.1	9.7
2002	4.3	10.1
2003	4.5	10.5
2004	4.7	10.8
2005	4.9	10.9
2006	4.9	10.6
2007	4.9	10.6
2008	4.9	10.4
2009	4.9	10.6
2010	4.8	9.8
2011	4.9	10.2
2012	4.8	10.0

Source: Based on a CRS analysis of data provided by the U.S. Department of Justice, Bureau of Prisons.

Notes: Ratios were calculated using figures on the number of inmates held in BOP facilities at the end of the fiscal year.

While it might appear somewhat surprising that the BOP would have an inmate-to-correctional officer ratio that was twice the ratio of inmates to staff—especially since the data presented above indicate that state correctional agencies have inmate-to-correctional officer ratios that are much closer to inmate-to-staff ratios—the BOP trains all of its staff as correctional officers, which means that the bureau does not need as many correctional officers to maintain the same level of security as other correctional agencies. For example, in many state prisons it would not be uncommon for a correctional officer to be stationed in a classroom while an instructor was teaching a class. However, since all staff in BOP facilities have been trained as correctional officers, the BOP does not place a correctional officer in classrooms during instructional periods.

A review of BOP staffing levels by the GAO suggests that federal prison facilities might be understaffed. The GAO cites a DOJ study from August 2010 that concluded that nearly all BOP facilities had fewer correctional officers on staff than needed.[64] The GAO noted that with the exception of hiring staff when a new facility opens, the number of staff positions has generally not increased as the prison population has increased, which is reflected by the slow, but relatively steady, increase in the inmate-to-staff ratio (the GAO reported that the inmate-to-staff ratio in FY1997 was 3.6:1).[65] The GAO reported that staffing in BOP facilities is, on average, less than 90% of authorized levels. The fact that the inmate-to-staff ratio has increased while the inmate-to-

---

[64] GAO prison crowding report, p. 23.

[65] Ibid., p. 22.

correctional officer ratio has remained fairly steady might be the result of the way that wardens make staffing decisions. The BOP funds staffing levels to the extent possible after the costs of caring for the inmate population (e.g., food, clothing, and medical care) are met. A warden might choose to use his or her allotted funding to fill more correctional officers positions while leaving more support staff positions unfilled. The overall inmate-to-staff ratio, which includes staff in the BOP's central office and regional offices, might mask staffing issues experienced by individual facilities. The GAO reported that the BOP calculates a ratio of inmates to institutional staff. From FY2006 to FY2011, the inmate to total institutional staff ratio for all facilities and for all male facilities was approximately 5.2:1. Also, the overall inmate-to-staff and inmate-to-correctional officer ratios do not reflect the fact that those ratios can vary based on the type of institution, the time of day, and the day of the week.[66] For example, the inmate-to-correctional officer ratio might be higher in low-security facilities compared to medium- and high-security facilities (though, arguably, this should be expected because lower security inmates should require less supervision). In addition, the inmate-to-correctional officer ratio might be lower during the night shift than during the day shifts.

The GAO also reported that staffing levels might be affected by some identified recruitment challenges the BOP faces. For example, some BOP officials reported that they have had problems with finding enough qualified candidates.[67] Furthermore, officials have reported problems with hiring professional staff (e.g., psychologists or medical staff) because BOP salaries were less than those paid for similar work in the surrounding community.[68]

---

[66] Ibid. pp. 23-24.

[67] Ibid., p. 22.

[68] Ibid.

Figure 12. Change in BOP Staff, Correctional Officers, and Institutional Inmate Population

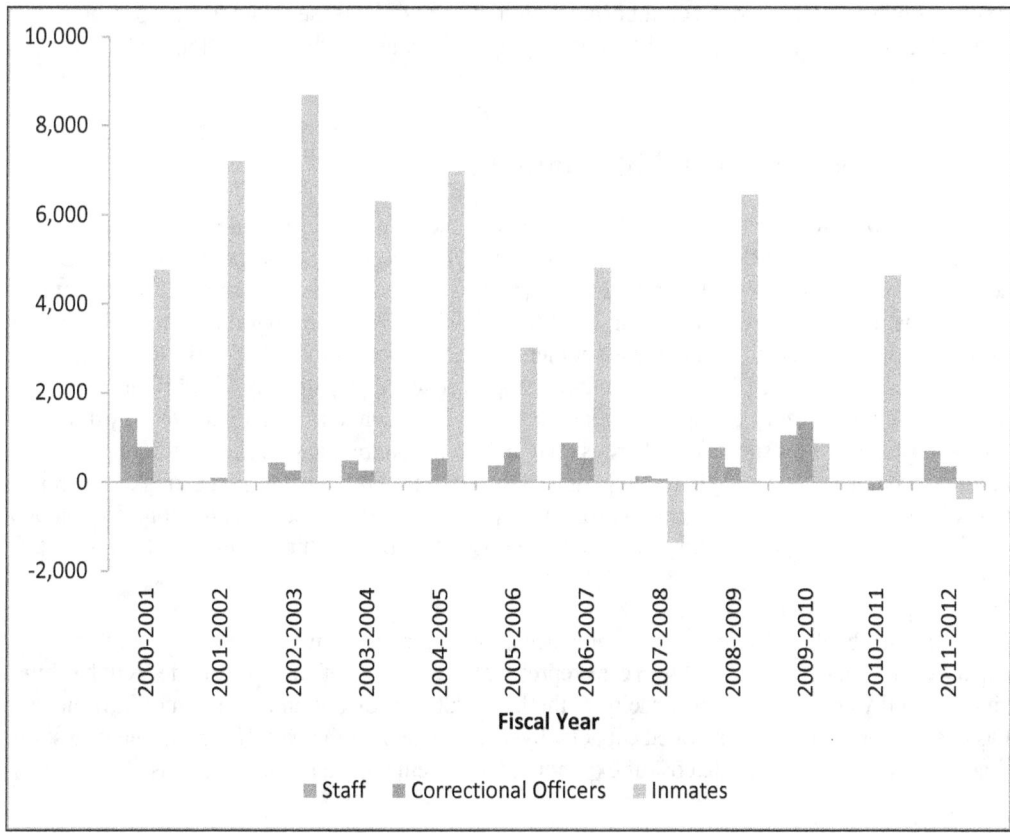

Source: Based on a CRS analysis of data provided by the U.S. Department of Justice, Bureau of Prisons.

Notes: Changes in the inmate population is only for inmates incarcerated in BOP facilities, not the total inmate population which would include inmates held in private facilities.

The data also show that in order to bring down either the inmate-to-staff ratio or the inmate-to-correctional officer ratio, there would have to be a significant increase in the BOP's S&E appropriation relative to the growth in the size of the federal prison population.[69]

Inmate-to-staff ratios might be an issue for Congress because it could mean that BOP facilities are less secure. In the research conducted by the BOP that evaluated causes of inmate misconduct (discussed above), the BOP estimated that a one-inmate increase in a prison's inmate-to-staff ratio increased the prison's annual serious assault rate by 4.5 assaults per 5,000 inmates.[70] In addition, more inmates per staff member could mean less access to rehabilitative programming because higher inmate-to-staff ratios could mean that BOP would not have the resources to meet the increasing demand for education, substance abuse treatment, and other rehabilitative programs. Through the Second Chance Act of 2007 (P.L. 110-199), Congress has required the BOP to help

---

[69] For more information on how the BOP's appropriations are split between decision units and what funding under those decision units is used for, see CRS Report R42486, *The Bureau of Prisons (BOP): Operations and Budget*, by Nathan James.

[70] *The Effects of Changing Crowding and Staffing Levels in Federal Prisons on Inmate Violence Rates.*

prepare inmates for re-entry, and the BOP has identified rehabilitative programming as a key component of its re-entry strategy for federal inmates.[71] Therefore, if the BOP does not have the resources to hire staff at a rate commensurate with the rate of increase in the federal prison population, the BOP might not be able to fully prepare inmates for their transition back to the community.

Prison Construction and Maintenance

Funds for new prison construction and expansion and the modernization and repair of existing facilities come from BOP's Buildings and Facilities (B&F) account. Appropriations for the B&F account have fluctuated over the past 32 fiscal years. Congress made a substantial investment in prison construction and expansion from FY1989-FY1992, with an appropriation of nearly $3 billion for the B&F account. There was another spike in appropriations for the B&F account between FY1999 and FY2004, when Congress appropriated approximately $3.4 billion. A comparison of the history of appropriations for the B&F account and historical overcrowding levels in BOP facilities shows that there is a lag between Congress appropriating funding for additional bedspace and a reduction in prison overcrowding. This is because it can take several years for the BOP to identify a location for a new prison, award the contracts for construction of the facility, complete construction, and bring the prison "online" by hiring new employees to staff the facility.

Data provided by the BOP indicate that it is becoming more expensive to expand federal prison capacity. The data presented in **Figure 13** represent the total cost of each prison the BOP has built since 1994 divided by the rated capacity of the facility; this provides an indication of how much it has cost the BOP to expand its rated capacity by one inmate over the past 18 years. The data show that, in general, the per inmate cost of expanding the system's rated capacity increased.

---

[71] BOP's FY2013 S&E Budget Justification, p. 33.

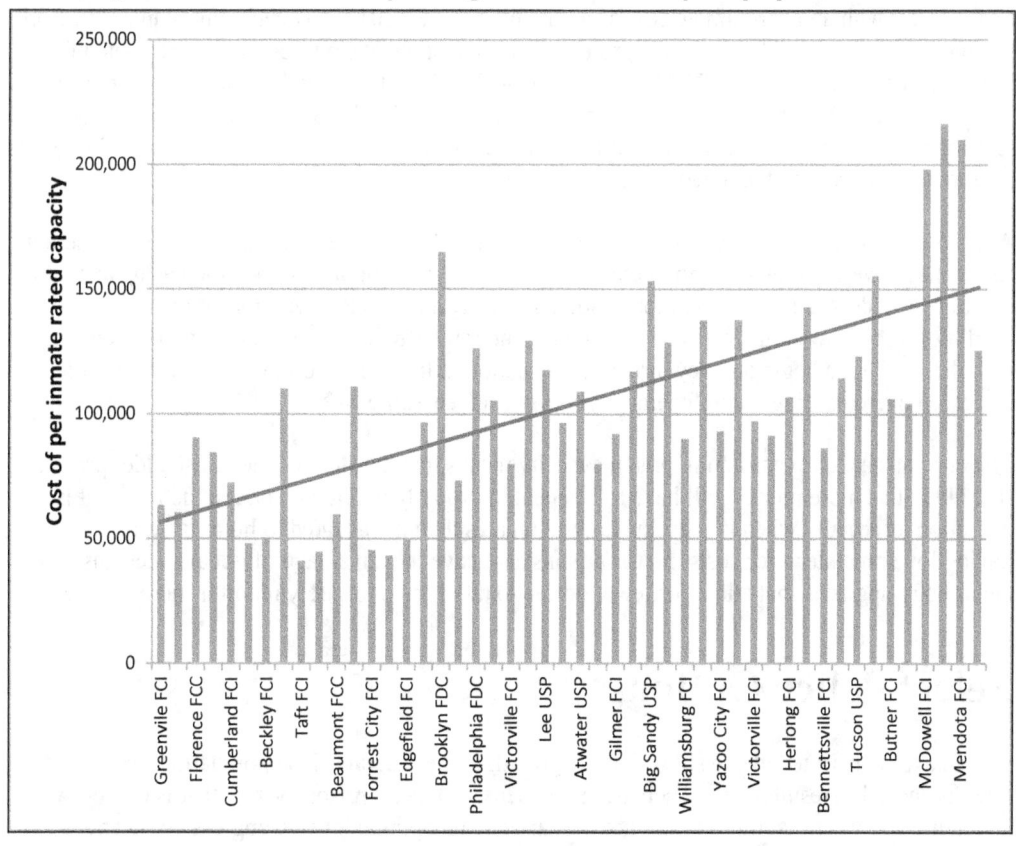

Figure 13. The Cost of Expanding Rated Prison Capacity by One Inmate

Source: Based on a CRS analysis of data provided by the U.S. Department of Justice, Bureau of Prisons.

Notes: Each bar in **Figure 13** represents the total cost of building a new prison divided by the number of beds in the completed prison. The data are presented in chronological order, with the first bar on the left (Greenville FCI) representing a facility completed in 1994 and the last bar on the right (Aliceville FCI; not labeled) representing a facility completed in 2011.

The growing prison population and related overcrowding is contributing to the deterioration of the BOP's facilities. As discussed above, the B&F account, in addition to providing funding for prison construction, also provides funding for the maintenance of the BOP's prison facilities. The BOP currently operates 117 prison facilities, and approximately one-third of those facilities are more than 50 years old.[72] Moreover, failure to perform adequate maintenance on existing facilities can result in larger capital investment in future years as prisons and utility systems deteriorate and, according to the BOP, can cause direct and/or indirect security problems.[73] According to the BOP, some prisons are experiencing "extensive wear and tear, as well as premature deterioration" because the facilities are holding more inmates than they were originally designed to hold.[74] The BOP reports that it has a backlog of 154 modernization and repair (M&R)

---

[72] U.S. Department of Justice, Bureau of Prisons, *FY2013 Performance Budget, Congressional Submission, Buildings and Facilities*, p. 5, http://www.justice.gov/jmd/2013justification/pdf/fy13-bop-bf-justification.pdf.

[73] Ibid.

[74] Ibid., p. 23.

projects with an approximate cost of $349 million for FY2012,[75] which is up from a backlog of 134 projects with an approximate cost of $302 million in FY2011.[76] The amount required to work through the current backlog of M&R projects is more than what Congress has appropriated for M&R projects going back to FY1999 (see **Table A-2**). The estimate only reflects "major" projects (repairs costing $300,000 or more) that have been approved by the BOP's administration for funding when appropriations are available. As such, the $349 million estimate probably does not capture the full extent of all needed repairs.

Appropriations for the B&F account have enabled the BOP to expand bedspace at a rate where it can manage overcrowding but not reduce it. The federal prison population is increasing at a rate where new bedspace is accounted for as soon as it is available. However, recent reductions in funding for the New Construction decision unit under the B&F account mean that the BOP will lack the funding to begin any new prison construction in the near future, which could result in increased overcrowding in the federal prison system (see **Table A-2**).

The current state of expansion in prison capacity means that the BOP cannot close older prisons. It is likely that more money will have to be spent to properly maintain a prison the longer it is in operation, especially when it is housing more inmates than it was rated to hold. In addition to having lower maintenance costs, newer prisons also have the advantage of updated designs and technology upgrades that allow for fewer correctional officers to safely monitor more inmates.

Select Policy Options

The analyses presented above show that the growth in the federal prison population over the past three decades has resulted in an increasingly expensive federal prison system that is overcrowded and aging and where facilities might not be staffed at an optimal level. Congress could choose to address the mounting number of federal inmates either in the context of existing correctional policies or by changing the current policies. Specific policy options under these two courses are discussed in more detail below.

Continuing or Expanding Current Correctional Policies

Under the umbrella of continuing existing policies, Congress could consider addressing issues related to the burgeoning federal prison population by (1) expanding the capacity of the federal prison system, (2) continuing to invest in rehabilitative programming, (3) placing more inmates in private correctional facilities, or some combination of the three.

Expanding the Capacity of the Federal Prison System

Arguably one of the most straightforward approaches for managing the steadily increasing number of federal inmates is to expand the capacity of the federal prison system. Congress could choose to mitigate some issues related to federal prison population growth by appropriating more funding so the BOP could expand prison capacity to alleviate overcrowding, update and properly

---

[75] Ibid., p. 27.

[76] U.S. Department of Justice, Bureau of Prisons, *FY2012 Performance Budget, Congressional Submission, Buildings and Facilities*, p. 25, http://www.justice.gov/jmd/2012justification/pdf/fy12-bop-bf-justification.pdf.

maintain existing facilities, and hire additional staff. While a large-scale expansion of the federal prison system might help reduce overcrowding, it takes several years for a prison to be built and be ready to accept inmates, so if Congress chooses to appropriate funding for an expansion of the BOP's infrastructure, it could be several years before overcrowding is reduced. Even if the federal prison population stabilized at the current level, the BOP would have to add over 50,000 additional beds in order to eliminate overcrowding. The BOP projects the federal prison population to increase to nearly 250,000 inmates by FY2018.[77] These projections are based on what has happened in the past, and as discussed above, the federal prison population has been increasing for more than 30 years. Should Congress choose to invest in a wide-scale expansion of prison capacity, and the prison population decreases in the future, the surplus bedspace could allow the BOP to close some of its older facilities, which, in general, require more maintenance and need higher inmate-to-staff ratios to safely operate.

Critics contend that expanding the capacity of the federal prison system does not address the continued growth of the federal prison population. Also, this policy option would not resolve the issue of the rising cost of the federal prison system; in fact, it could exacerbate it. However, alternatives that would reduce the federal prison population would most likely involve prosecuting fewer people in federal courts, providing ways for inmates to be released before they served a significant proportion of their sentences, putting more inmates into diversionary programs, or placing more offenders on some form of community supervision. If Congress does not wish to take any of these steps, a large-scale expansion of the federal prison system might be the sole way to manage the effects of an increasing prison population. Some may argue that in order to protect public safety Congress should appropriate the funding necessary to expand the federal prison system rather than adopt policy changes that would reduce the prison population through early releases, alternatives to incarceration, or fewer prosecutions.

Investing in Rehabilitative Programs

A review of the literature on rehabilitative programs (e.g., academic and vocational education, cognitive-behavioral programs, and both community- and prison-based drug treatment) suggests that there are enough scientifically sound evaluations to conclude that they are effective at reducing recidivism, which could potentially help stem growth in the federal prison population in the future.[78] The BOP offers a variety of rehabilitation programs such as academic and vocational education, work programs through the Federal Prison Industries (FPI), substance abuse treatment, and cognitive-behavioral programs that focus on promoting pro-social behavior.[79] One possible option for reducing the federal prison population would be to ensure that the BOP has the resources it needs to provide rehabilitative services to inmates.

At a time when some policymakers are considering reducing discretionary funding for federal agencies, there might be some effort to restrain the growth of the BOP's appropriations, including for rehabilitative services. The BOP has to administer the federal prison system within the funds appropriated for it by Congress. As shown in **Figure 9**, the per capita cost of providing

---

[77] U.S. Department of Justice, Bureau of Prisons, FY2012 Performance Budget, Congressional Submission, Salaries and Expenses, p. 2, http://www.justice.gov/jmd/2012justification/pdf/fy12-bop-se-justification.pdf.

[78] Doris Layton MacKenzie, *What Works in Corrections: Reducing the Criminal Activities of Offenders and Delinquents* (New York: Cambridge University Press, 2006), pp. 331-333, hereinafter, "*What Works in Corrections.*"

[79] For more information on the BOP's rehabilitative programs see CRS Report R41525, *Federal Prison Inmates: Rehabilitative Needs and Program Participation*, by Nathan James.

rehabilitative programming for inmates has been increasing. If the BOP does not have sufficient resources, it might not be able to provide rehabilitative programming to all inmates who need it. The federal prison population has continued to grow, and unless there is a change in the trend over the past 30 years, it would appear likely that there will be a growing need for and cost of rehabilitative programming in the federal prison system.

It could be argued that in order to reduce the growing cost of operating the federal prison system, the BOP should reduce funding for rehabilitative programming and invest solely in providing for the subsistence of inmates and maintaining a level of staffing that is adequate to ensure that federal prisons are secure. However, reducing programming opportunities might result in more inmate idleness, which might result in more inmate misconduct. Moreover, as noted above, the BOP is authorized to reduce an inmate's sentence by up to one year for successfully completing a residential substance abuse treatment program; therefore, reducing programming opportunities could hamper one of the few avenues the BOP has for releasing inmates early. It is also possible that BOP might be able to realize some long-term cost savings by successfully rehabilitating inmates. For example, research by the Washington State Institute for Public Policy (WSIPP) suggests that effective rehabilitation programs can result in cost savings.[80]

As policymakers consider the appropriate level of funding for the BOP in light of concerns about the federal deficit and potential freezes or reductions in non-defense discretionary spending, they could consider whether it is prudent to increase resources for the BOP's rehabilitative programs in the near-term in order to realize potential long-term benefits. As outlined above, the BOP's appropriations have increased along with the federal prison population. Yet, current funding may be inadequate for the BOP to provide more rehabilitative opportunities to federal inmates. The size of the effect that decreased recidivism amongst federal offenders would have on the BOP's budget would depend on how many new inmates the BOP incarcerates. If new commitments exceed the number of inmates released who do not return to prison then the demand for prisons, personnel, and inmate programs and services would continue to grow, although possibly at a slower rate. If the number of new commitments is less than the number of inmates released who do not return to prison then the demand for prisons, personnel, and inmate programs and services would decrease. However, even if the growth of the federal prison population slows, the demand for increased BOP appropriations may continue.

Placing More Inmates in Private Prisons

The BOP has placed an increasing share of federal inmates in contract facilities as a way of managing the growth in the federal prison population. Congress might also consider whether *more* federal inmates should be housed in private facilities as a means of reducing crowding in federal prisons and potentially reducing the cost of operating the federal prison system. The number of inmates under the BOP's jurisdiction held in contract facilities has steadily increased since the early 1980s, and the BOP expects the trend to continue into the later part of this decade. However, the growth in the number of inmates held in contract facilities is mostly the result of more inmates being placed in Residential Reentry Centers (RRCs) at the end of their sentences. Most BOP inmates held in private correctional facilities are low-level, non-citizen offenders. The debate about whether to house inmates in privately operated correctional facilities has been

---

[80] Steve Aos, Marna Miller, and Elizabeth Drake, *Evidence-based Public Policy Options to Reduce Future Prison Construction, Criminal Justice Costs, and Crime Rates*, Washington State Institute for Public Policy, Olympia, WA, October 2006, http://www.wsipp.wa.gov/rptfiles/06-10-1201.pdf.

framed by two overarching questions: (1) can private facilities incarcerate inmates at a lower cost and (2) can private facilities provide services that are equal or superior to the services provided in public institutions?

The BOP attempted to answer these questions, at the behest of Congress, by operating the Taft Correctional Institution (TCI) as a private facility as a part of a privatization demonstration project.[81] The BOP awarded a contract to the Geo Group (formerly Wackenhut Corrections Corporation) to operate the facility from 1997 to 2007.[82] The BOP, through the National Institute of Justice, funded an evaluation of TCI and three similar BOP facilities,[83] which was conducted by Abt Associates, Inc. In addition, the BOP's Office of Research, in conjunction with the Center for Naval Analyses (CNA) Corporation, conducted its own evaluation of TCI and the similar facilities. Both the Abt and BOP evaluations found that TCI was cheaper to operate on a per diem basis than the three comparable facilities, but the two evaluations offer different conclusions as to how much was saved by operating TCI as a private institution. The Abt analysis concluded that the average per diem cost of incarceration for the three BOP-operated facilities in FY1999 was 18.9% greater than the per diem cost of incarceration for TCI; in FY2000 it was 20.0% greater; in FY2001 it was 17.5% greater; and in FY2002 it was 14.8% greater.[84] In comparison, the BOP analysis concluded that the average per diem cost of incarceration for the three BOP-operated facilities in FY1999 was 4.0% greater than the per diem cost of incarceration for TCI; in FY2000 it was 5.4% greater; in FY2001 it was 0.3% greater; and in FY2002 it was 2.2% greater.[85] The two primary reasons for the different conclusions are economies of scale[86] realized by TCI and differences in how per diem rates were calculated.[87] TCI had on average 300 more inmates each year than the three BOP-operated prisons, which means that TCI was able to take advantage of economies of scale that decreased average costs. In the BOP analysis, the researchers adjusted for these economies of scale by estimating what expenditures would have been for the BOP facilities if they had prison populations similar to TCI. In addition, the Abt analysis assumed that the BOP would not provide many resources to support TCI's operations, resulting in a large amount of savings from reduced indirect overhead costs. The BOP analysis assumed that the BOP would continue to incur some overhead expenses related to overseeing TCI. As such, the BOP included a 10-12% overhead rate in its analysis.

Research that reviewed the results of state and local efforts to privatize correctional systems generally found that it is questionable whether privatization can deliver lower costs and whether

---

[81] The conference report (H.Rept. 104-863) for the Omnibus Consolidated Appropriations Act, 1997 (P.L. 104-208) incorporates, by reference, language from the Senate report (S.Rept. 104-353) to accompany the Senate committee-reported version of H.R. 3814 (104th Congress), that requires the BOP to undertake "a 5-year prison privatization demonstration project" involving the facility that the BOP built in Taft, CA.

[82] The Taft Correctional Institution is still operating as a private facility. After the contract with the Geo Group expired in 2007, the contract was recompeted and it was awarded to Management and Training Corporation.

[83] The three similar facilities included in the evaluation were FCI Yazoo City, FCI Elkton, and FCI Forrest City.

[84] Gerry Gaes, "Cost, Performance Studies Look at Prison Privatization," *NIJ Journal*, no. 259 (March 2008), p. 33.

[85] Ibid.

[86] "Economies of scale" generally refers to the increase in efficiency of production that accompanies expanded production. In economic terms, this means that the average cost of the good produced decreases and production increases because fixed costs are shared over an increased number of goods. In terms of the BOP evaluation of TCI, "economies of scale" would refer to the decreased per prisoner costs resulting from spreading the prison's operating costs over a greater number of inmates.

[87] Ibid., p. 34.

services provided by private prisons are comparable to services provided by public prisons.[88] One of the first studies to quantitatively summarize the results of several evaluations of prison privatization efforts found that regardless of whether the prison was privately or publicly operated, the economies of scale, the prison's age, and the prison's security level were the most significant determinants of the daily per diem cost.[89] The researchers concluded that "[a]lthough specific privatization policy alternatives may result in modest cost savings...relinquishing the responsibility of managing prisons to the private sphere is unlikely to alleviate much of the financial burden on state correctional budgets."[90] Their conclusions are echoed by a review of the literature on privatization. In this analysis, the researchers concluded "that prison privatization provides neither a clear advantage nor disadvantage compared with publicly managed prisons. Neither cost savings nor improvements in quality of confinement are guaranteed through privatization."[91] However, even though both studies limited their analyses to the most methodologically sound evaluations, these evaluations are still limited to the same issues described above, namely, what costs are considered when the evaluators calculated whether privatization could lower correctional costs. As discussed above, these assumptions can have a considerable effect on the results of the evaluation.

Placing more inmates in private facilities could help alleviate overcrowding in federal prisons without the need to invest in a large-scale expansion of federal prison bedspace. Expanding capacity through contracting for additional bedspace rather than building new prisons could give Congress the flexibility to reduce capacity if the federal prison population decreased in the future. However, research suggests that moving federal prisoners into private prisons might not help to control the rising costs of the federal prison system. Also, medium and high security facilities are the most crowded, and the BOP is less inclined to place medium and high security inmates in private facilities. Congress might also consider whether it wants to place a greater portion of the federal prison population in the custody of private operators when the BOP has less direct oversight over the day-to-day operations of private facilities.

Changing Existing Correctional and Sentencing Policies to Reduce the Prison Population

Policymakers might also consider whether they want to revise some of the changes that have been made to federal criminal justice policy over the past three decades. A confluence of these changes has resulted in an increasing number of offenders being sent to federal prisons. Should Congress decide to change federal criminal justice policy to try to reduce the number of inmates held in federal prisons, policymakers might start by considering which offenders are incarcerated and the length of their sentences.

---

[88] Travis C. Pratt and Jeff Maahs, "Are Private Prisons More Cost-effective Than Public Prisons? A Meta-analysis of Evaluation Research Studies," *Crime and Delinquency*, vol. 45, no. 3 (July 1999), pp. 358-371; Dina Perrone and Travis C. Pratt, "Comparing the Quality of Confinement and Cost-effectiveness of Public Versus Private Prisons: What We Know, Why We Do Not Know More, and Where to Go From Here," *The Prison Journal*, vol. 83, no. 3 (September 2003), pp. 301-322; Brad W. Lundahl, Chelsea Kunz, and Cyndi Brownell, et al., "A Meta-analysis of Cost and Quality of Confinement Indicators," *Research on Social Work Practice*, vol. 19, no. 4 (July 2009), pp. 383-394.

[89] Travis C. Pratt and Jeff Maahs, "Are Private Prisons More Cost-effective Than Public Prisons? A Meta-analysis of Evaluation Research Studies," *Crime and Delinquency*, vol. 45, no. 3 (July 1999), p. 367.

[90] Ibid., pp. 367-368.

[91] Brad W. Lundahl, Chelsea Kunz, and Cyndi Brownell, et al., "A Meta-analysis of Cost and Quality of Confinement Indicators," *Research on Social Work Practice*, vol. 19, no. 4 (July 2009), p. 392.

Changes to Mandatory Minimum Penalties

As discussed earlier, the USSC concluded that, in part, mandatory minimum penalties have contributed to the growing federal prison population. It might be argued that some or all mandatory minimum penalties should be repealed as a way to manage the growth of the federal prison population. Allowing defendants to be sentenced using the federal sentencing guidelines could allow for more individualized sentencing, thereby allowing the court to mete out punishment using an array of variables that reflect a more nuanced analysis of a defendant's culpability. Opponents of widespread use of mandatory minimum penalties contend that they are a blunt instrument with which to determine a proper sentence. The USSC reported that "certain mandatory minimum provisions apply too broadly, are set too high, or both, to warrant the prescribed minimum penalty for the full range of offenders who could be prosecuted under the particular criminal statute."[92] Also, to the extent that mandatory minimum penalties have contributed to sentence inflation as a result of the USSC incorporating them into the federal sentencing guidelines, repealing some mandatory minimum penalties might reduce the amount of time inmates serve in federal prison.

However, proponents of the continued use of mandatory minimum penalties contend that after the Supreme Court's ruling in *United States v. Booker*[93] and its progeny (e.g., *Gall v. United States*[94] and *Kimbrough v. United States*[95]), which rendered the sentencing guidelines effectively advisory, Congress has a responsibility to set minimum penalties for some offenses as a way to limit judicial discretion, thereby preventing unwanted sentencing disparities. It has been argued that mandatory minimum penalties promote uniformity and fairness for defendants, transparent and predictable outcomes, and a higher level of truth and integrity in sentencing.[96] Also, should Congress choose to repeal some or all mandatory minimum penalties, policymakers would relinquish their ability to control the amount of time inmates serve for certain offenses.

Even if Congress chooses not to repeal any mandatory minimum sentences, policymakers could review current mandatory minimum penalties to ensure that they are (1) not excessively severe, (2) narrowly tailored to apply only to those offenders who warrant such punishment, and (3) applied consistently.[97]

Alternatives to Incarceration

During the 1980s many states instituted a series of alternatives to incarceration as a way to respond to an increasing number of convicted offenders and wide-scale prison overcrowding.[98] Prior to this, sentencing options were limited to incarceration or probation. However, there was growing sentiment that some crimes were too severe to be punished by placing the offender on

---

[92] *Mandatory Minimum Penalties in the Federal Criminal Justice System*, p. 345.

[93] 543 U.S. 220 (2005).

[94] 552 U.S. 38 (2007).

[95] 552 U.S. 85 (2007).

[96] Erik Luna and Paul G. Cassell, "Mandatory Minimalism," *Cardozo Law Review*, vol. 32, no. 1 (September 2010), p. 11.

[97] *Mandatory Minimum Penalties in the Federal Criminal Justice System*, p. 368.

[98] *What Works in Corrections*, p. 304.

probation, but those same crimes were not severe enough to warrant incarceration. Therefore, states started to develop a series of alternative sentences that fell somewhere between probation and incarceration. These alternatives included house arrest, electronic monitoring, intensive supervision, boot camps, split sentences, day reporting centers, fines, and community service.[99] The programs provide graduated sanctions that might be more appropriate than either probation or incarceration, and provided a higher level of offender restraint and accountability than traditional probation. Some also provide higher levels of treatment or services for problems such as substance abuse, low education levels, and unemployment.

A majority of the evaluations of intensive supervision and electronic monitoring programs found that there was no significant difference in recidivism rates between offenders sentenced to alternatives to incarceration and offenders in control groups.[100] This means that increasing surveillance and control of offenders' activities does not decrease their criminal activities. Ironically, while these programs were created as a means of reducing the number of incarcerated individuals, the increased surveillance might increase the probability that violations of the terms of probation will be detected, which could increase the number of inmates as probationers are often incarcerated for technical violations. One shortcoming of the research is that since most intensive supervision programs increase the probability of detection, there is no way to tell if the underlying level of criminality changed between the treatment and control groups, i.e., the increased probability of detection might mean that offenders in the control group are simply more likely to be caught when they commit crimes, even though offenders in the control group commit crime at the same, or even higher, rate. Also, the research tended to focus on whether the restraining aspects of the program could reduce recidivism. Some evaluations found that inmates who received treatment while participating in an intensive supervision program were less likely to be arrested.[101]

Placing More Inmates on Probation

Congress could consider whether there are alternative ways to properly manage offenders convicted of committing relatively minor crimes without sending them to prison. Data from BJS show that in FY2010 over half of inmates entering federal prison were sentenced to three years or less. Given the relatively short sentences these inmates received, it is likely that they were sentenced for relatively minor offenses. One policy option Congress could consider is amending penalties for some offenses to allow more defendants to be placed on probation rather than being sentenced to a period of incarceration. However, the *Booker* decision that rendered the federal sentencing guidelines advisory might influence any debate Congress would have over who would be placed on probation. The sentencing guidelines placed substantial restrictions on when courts could sentence defendants to probation. Under §5B1.1 of the sentencing guidelines, defendants can only be placed on probation if their sentence under the guidelines is equal to or less than 15 months. Nonetheless, after the Supreme Court's ruling in *Booker*, federal judges are not required to impose a sentence within the range calculated under the sentencing guidelines. Therefore, judges can impose probation for offenders unless (1) the defendant has been convicted of a class A or B felony,[102] (2) probation is statutorily precluded as a sentencing option, or (3) the defendant

---

[99] Ibid.

[100] Ibid., p. 306.

[101] Ibid., p. 318.

[102] A class A felony is an offense where the maximum term of imprisonment authorized is life imprisonment or death. A class B felony is an offense where the maximum term of imprisonment authorized is 25 years or more. 18 U.S.C. (continued...)

is sentenced to a term of imprisonment for the same or different offense that is not a petty offense.[103]

Data from the Administrative Office of the U.S. Courts suggest that in the post-*Booker* era courts have not chosen to sentence outside the guideline range to place more offenders on probation. Since the mid-1970s, a dwindling proportion of defendants sentenced for federal offenses were placed on probation (see **Figure 14**). The decrease in the proportion of sentenced defendants placed on probation coincides with the implementation of the federal sentencing guidelines. The data also show that the proportion of defendants that were placed on probation has further decreased since the *Booker* decision. Approximately 14% of defendants in FY2004 received probation; by FY2011, about 10% of defendants were placed on probation.

Data show that the risk of recidivism for probationers is the highest in the first year after being placed on probation.[104] It has been argued that surveillance and services should be front-loaded (i.e., more intensive at the beginning of a term of probation) to try to mitigate recidivism and other negative consequences that might occur during the first year that an offender is serving on probation.

A common argument from advocates of decreasing the use of incarceration is that it is cheaper to supervise an offender in the community than it is to incarcerate that individual. The Administrative Office of the U.S. Courts reports that the average annual cost of probation supervision was $3,938 per probationer.[105] In comparison, the average annual cost of incarceration for FY2010 was $25,627 per inmate. However, some of the lower cost of probation relative to incarceration might be the result of fewer and lower-risk offenders being placed on probation. It is possible that the annual cost of probation would increase if Congress expanded the number of people placed on probation and implemented some of the changes discussed below.

(...continued)

§3559(a).

[103] 18 U.S.C. §3561(a).

[104] Ibid., p. 519.

[105] Administrative Office of the U.S. Courts, "Newly Available: Costs of Incarceration and Supervision in FY 2010," press release, June 23, 2011, http://www.uscourts.gov/news/newsview/11-06-23/ Newly_Available_Costs_of_Incarceration_and_Supervision_in_FY_2010.aspx.

**Figure 14. Proportion of Sentenced Defendants in Federal Courts
Placed on Probation**

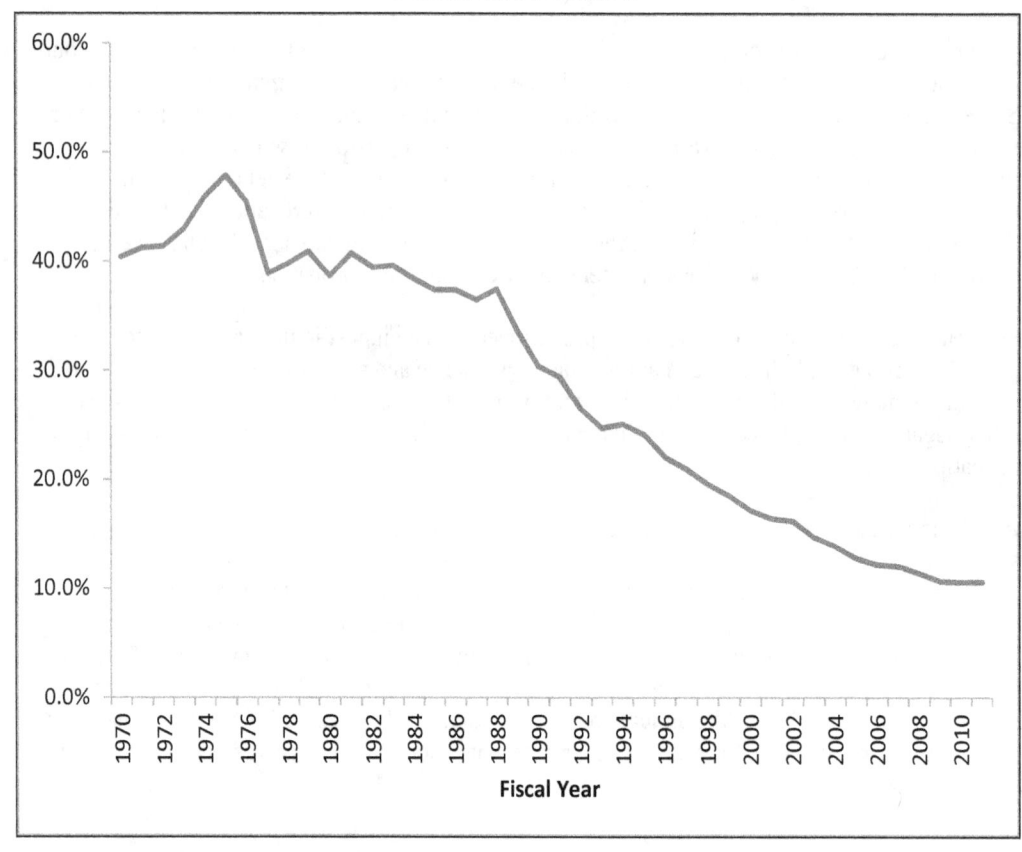

Source: FY1970-FY1996 data taken from *Sourcebook of Criminal Justice Statistics, 1996*, Table 5.27. Data for FY1997-FY2011 taken from *Judicial Business of the U.S. Courts* for each respective fiscal year.

Should Congress choose to expand probation as a sentencing option for more offenses, research suggests that probation programs that use a validated risk assessment tool to sort offenders into high- and low-risk groups and focus resources and supervision on higher-risk offenders might be more effective at reducing recidivism.[106] Research also suggests that probation programs that offer a mix of evidence-based treatment that is delivered to offenders who are the most likely to benefit from it along with surveillance are more effective at reducing recidivism than surveillance-only probation.[107] As one expert noted, "'[t]reatment' alone is not enough, nor is 'surveillance' by itself adequate. Programs that can increase offender-to-officer contact *and* [emphasis original] provide treatment have reduced recidivism."[108] Researchers have found that participants in probation programs that subject probationers with substance abuse issues to frequent random drug testing and that require probationers who violate the terms of their probation to serve intermediate sanctions, such as a short stay in jail, are less likely to recidivate

---

[106] Joan Petersilia, "Community Corrections: Probation, Parole, and Prisoner Reentry," in *Crime and Public Policy*, ed. James Q. Wilson and Joan Petersilia (New York: Oxford University Press, 2011), pp. 521-522, hereinafter, "Community Corrections: Probation, Parole, and Prisoner Reentry."

[107] Ibid., p. 522.

[108] Ibid.

than those who were on regular probation.[109] Another option Congress might consider is allowing probationers who strictly adhere to their conditions of probation to be released early. Research has shown that an earned discharge strategy can reduce recidivism.[110]

Expanding the Use of Residential Reentry Centers

Congress could also consider extending the BOP's authority to place inmates with short sentences who are deemed to be low security risks directly into Residential Reentry Centers (RRCs, i.e., halfway houses). A *New York Times* (*Times*) investigation of halfway houses in New Jersey might raise some questions amongst policymakers about whether placing some federal inmates in RRCs rather than federal prisons is a viable policy option. Like the BOP, the New Jersey Department of Corrections contracts with private halfway houses to give inmates the opportunity to reestablish themselves in society before being released from custody. The *Times* investigation found that approximately 5,100 inmates have escaped since 2005 and that some inmates have committed new offenses after they escaped.[111] However, many escaped inmates were captured or returned within hours or days.[112] The *Times* also uncovered instances of lax security because counselors were either poorly trained, outnumbered, or feared for their safety; inmate-on-inmate violence; and questionably delivered rehabilitative services.[113]

The Department of Justice's Office of the Inspector General (OIG) completed an audit of six RRCs[114] that the BOP had contracts with to determine whether the RRCs operations were conducted in compliance with the BOP's requirements and whether the BOP effectively administers and monitors RRC contracts.[115] The OIG's audit included a review of the files of 177 inmates who were transferred to one of the six RRCs between FY2008 and FY2010. The OIG concluded that the RRCs adequately met most Statement of Work (SOW)[116] requirements; however, the six RRCs did not fully comply with conditions related to substance abuse testing, escapes, and authorized inmate absences. Specifically, the OIG found that 30% of the inmates with histories of substance abuse did not have documentation showing that they were given required drug tests.[117] The OIG found that from FY2008 to FY2010, approximately 3% of the

---

[109] Kevin McEvoy, "HOPE: A Swift and Certain Process for Probationers," *NIJ Journal*, no. 269 (March 2012), p. 17.

[110] Community Corrections: Probation, Parole, and Prisoner Reentry, p. 524.

[111] Sam Dolnick, "As Escapees Stream Out, a Penal Business Thrives," *New York Times*, June 17, 2012, p. A1.

[112] Ibid., p. A16.

[113] Sam Dolnick, "Poorly Staffed, a Halfway House in New Jersey is Mired in Chaos," *New York Times*, June 18, 2012; Sam Dolnick, "At Penal Unit, A Volatile Mix Fuels a Murder," *New York Times*, June 19, 2012.

[114] The RRCs were located in Denver, CO; Leavenworth, KS; El Paso, TX; Boston, MA; Washington, DC; and Kansas City, MO.

[115] U.S. Department of Justice, Office of the Inspector General, *Audit of the Federal Bureau of Prisons' Contracting for and Management of Residential Reentry Centers*, Audit Report 12-20, Washington , DC, March 2012, p. 5, http://www.justice.gov/oig/reports/2012/a1220.pdf.

[116] The Statement of Work (SOW) for RRCs is the primary document that outlines all of the BOP's requirements for contractors operating RRCs. The SOW requires RRCs to develop individualized program plans for each inmate that focus on, when applicable, reestablishing relationships with family, obtaining and maintaining employment, obtaining drug and alcohol abuse treatment, and finding housing. At the same time each RRC must: (1) be able to locate and verify the whereabouts of inmates at all times; (2) establish an surveillance program to deter and detect the illegal introduction of drugs and alcohol into the facility; (3) effectively discipline inmates; and (4) prepare and maintain required documentation. Ibid., p. 3.

[117] RRCs are required to randomly test at least 5% of all inmates for drugs and alcohol monthly, with a minimum of one inmate tested per month. In addition, an inmate with a known history of drug abuse, or who is suspected of illegal (continued...)

---

inmates transferred to the six RRCs included in the audit escaped.[118] In addition, the OIG found that 92 of the 177 inmates included in the audit had 434 authorized absences where they returned to the RRC more than one hour late, and no disciplinary action was taken or documented for 65 of the 71 inmates who returned more than one hour late with no reason for their tardiness.[119] The OIG also concluded that the BOP's monitoring procedures were sufficient to identify most RRC deficiencies related to compliance with the SOW and that corrective actions were implemented.

The *Times* investigation of halfway houses in New Jersey and the OIG's audit of RRCs might raise some potential issues for Congress. The *Times* report suggests that several of the problems experienced in the halfway houses that were the subject of its investigation resulted from the New Jersey Department of Corrections and local sheriffs' departments using halfway houses as a means of reducing prison and jail overcrowding, which resulted in inmates with violent histories and/or who were convicted for violent offenses being placed in halfway houses. These inmates were then supervised by employees with little training, who were not correctional officers and who, in some instances, feared the inmates because they were substantially outnumbered. This suggests that if Congress wanted to use RRCs as a way of reducing overcrowding in federal prisons that placement in RRCs should be limited to low-level, non-violent offenders. The *Times* article includes accounts from staff who reported fearing for their safety while patrolling the halfway houses at night because of lax security and high inmate-to-staff ratios. This might mean that should RRCs be used as a way to reduce the number of inmates held in federal prisons, the BOP will need to ensure that RRCs have properly trained and adequate staff and that the RRCs have satisfactory security measures in place. The findings from the OIG audit suggest that the BOP might need to increase its oversight of the RRCs it contracts with. This could mean that the BOP would need additional staff and an increase in its travel budget so BOP staff could make more frequent visits to RRCs.

If policymakers were concerned about whether RRCs are a valid alternative to placing some offenders in federal prison, Congress could choose to provide funding for a program that would allow the federal government to contract with local jails to provide short-term bedspace. One possible example is the Cooperative Agreement Program (CAP) whereby the U.S. Marshals Service (USMS) provided capital investment funding to local jails in exchange for guaranteed

---

(...continued)

drug use, must be tested no less than four times per month. RRCs are also required to give inmates a breathalyzer test every time they return from an unsupervised activity. Ibid., pp. 7-8.

[118] The OIG notes that there are three types of escapes: regular, technical new, and technical old. "Regular" escapes most closely fit the definition of what most would consider an escape. A regular escape is when an inmate fails to remain in RRC custody by (1) not reporting to the facility for admission at the scheduled time; (2) not remaining at the approved place of employment, training, or treatment during the hours specified by the terms of the employment, training, or treatment program; (3) not returning to the facility at the time prescribed; (4) not returning from an authorized furlough or pass at the time and place stipulated; (5) not abiding by conditions of employment, or curfew conditions of home confinement; or (6) leaving the facility without the permission of RRC staff. "Technical new" escapes occur when an inmate fails to remain in the RRC's custody by being arrested for a new charge. "Technical old" escapes occur when an inmate fails to remain in the RRC's custody by being arrested for an outstanding warrant while residing at a RRC. Of the escapes reported in the OIG's report, 75.3% were regular escapes, 12.7% were technical new escapes, and 11.9% were technical old escapes. Ibid. p. 15.

[119] RRCs can only authorize an inmate to leave for approved activities, including job searches, employment, religious services, and visitations with family and friends. Other than for employment or programming activities, such as drug abuse counseling, an inmate must generally be at the RRC facility from 9:00 p.m. to 6:00 a.m., unless the director has granted an exemption. RRCs are allowed to grant passes or furloughs to release inmates overnight or to travel distances of more than 100 miles. Ibid., pp. 18-19.

---

bedspace for federal detainees.[120] While the CAP was limited to securing bedspace for people in the custody of the USMS (i.e., people who have not yet been convicted of a crime), it is possible that the program could be expanded to allow the federal government to expand local jail capacity in order to secure bedspace for some lower-level federal inmates who are serving short sentences. It is likely that jails would be more secure than RRCs. In addition, jails are staffed by correctional officers, who might be better prepared to supervise federal inmates.

Allowing the BOP to confine more low-level inmates in RRCs would mean fewer inmates would be placed into already overcrowded facilities while still receiving a punishment for criminal behavior and supervision of their actions for a given period of time. However, FY2011 data published by the BOP show that per capita expenditures for RRCs ($26,163) were higher than the per capita cost of confining a prisoner in a minimum ($18,849), low ($23,780), or medium ($23,780) prison, so placing more low-level inmates in RRCs might not generate a substantial amount of savings.[121]

Congress could also consider whether to require courts to place certain offenders in RRCs for violating the terms of their supervised release rather than returning them to prison. As mentioned, the BOP might not save a significant amount of money by placing a greater number of inmates in RRCs, but by placing more of these short-term inmates in RRCs the BOP would have additional bedspace. In addition, the BOP would not have to invest time and money into re-processing the offender through the prison system.[122] This is not to suggest that all inmates who have their supervised release revoked would be suitable for RRC placement. Indeed, inmates who are arrested and/or convicted for serious offenses would most likely need to be placed in a secure facility. However, offenders who have their supervised release revoked for technical violations (e.g., repeatedly failing drug tests) might be suitable for placement in a less secure environment that still allows for monitoring of their actions.

All of the alternatives to incarceration discussed above place the offender in the community, which means there is some level of risk that the offender could commit new offenses, because even though the offender would be supervised, the level of supervision would most likely provide a lower level of control over the individual's actions than would be provided by correctional officers in a secure environment.

Early Release Measures

One possible way to reduce the growth of the federal prison population would be to expand the early release measures for federal inmates. There are several options Congress could consider if policymakers wanted to expand early release options for federal inmates, including (1) reinstating parole, (2) expanding good time credits, and (3) expanding the conditions under which courts could reduce sentences pursuant to 18 U.S.C. §3582(c)(1)(A).

---

[120] Funding for this program was discontinued after FY2004.

[121] See http://www.bop.gov/foia/fy11_per_capita_costs.pdf.

[122] For more information on how inmates are processed through the federal prison system, see CRS Report R42486, *The Bureau of Prisons (BOP): Operations and Budget*, by Nathan James.

Reinstating Parole

One option Congress might consider is whether to reinstate parole in the federal system. As discussed above, inmates sentenced for an offense in a federal court committed after November 1, 1987 are not eligible to be released on parole. Parole is one way correctional authorities can release inmates who are deemed to be at a low-risk for recidivism and place them in community supervision for the remainder of their sentences.

Should Congress consider reinstating parole for federal inmates, there are several salient issues that policymakers might think about. First, how would a parole system work within the current determinate sentencing structure used in federal courts? Traditionally, discretionary parole has been combined with an indeterminate sentencing structure (i.e., a system whereby the court could impose a sentence for a crime within a range prescribed in law). Indeterminate sentences allow the court to tailor sentences to each defendant, but this gave rise to concerns about whether some sentences were arbitrary and unfair. For example, two defendants who were convicted for similar crimes might receive different sentences depending on which judge happened to be presiding over their case. When combined with a parole board's discretion over when, if ever, someone would be granted parole, two defendants who were convicted of similar crimes could end up serving significantly different amounts of time in prison.

Congress sought to limit the discretion of the federal judiciary and the executive branch when it eliminated parole and replaced indeterminate sentencing with the sentencing guidelines. Parole might not be irreconcilable with a determinate sentencing structure. Courts could continue to use sentencing guidelines as a guidepost for determining a defendant's sentence and each inmate could then be eligible for parole after serving a certain portion of his or her sentence. However, should Congress allow federal inmates to be eligible for parole, it would grant the executive branch, through the U.S. Parole Commission (hereinafter, "commission"), some measure of control over determining how much time an inmate serves in prison. Congress might choose to limit some of the commission's discretion by setting a higher threshold for determining what portion of an inmate's sentence must be served before he or she is eligible to be placed on parole.[123]

Should Congress choose to reinstate parole for federal inmates, another key question would be whether eligibility would be made retroactive to inmates who were sentenced for federal crimes after November 1, 1987. As discussed above, approximately 3% of inmates currently incarcerated in federal facilities are still eligible for parole, which means that at the end of FY2011 there were nearly 204,600 inmates in federal prison who were not eligible for parole. Making eligibility for parole retroactive could potentially reduce the federal prison population in a shorter amount of time than it would if only newly convicted inmates were eligible for parole consideration. Data from the BOP indicate that nearly three-quarters of inmates have served at least 25% of their sentence, meaning that if Congress reinstated the old parole eligibility rules, a majority of federal

---

[123] Federal inmates who are eligible for parole (i.e., inmates sentenced before November 1, 1987) can be released after serving one-third of their sentences (if sentenced to a term of incarceration greater than one year) or after 10 years if sentenced to life or a term or incarceration over 30 years. However, the sentencing court could designate a minimum term of imprisonment the defendant would have to serve before being eligible for parole. The minimum term of imprisonment designated by the court could be less, but not more, than one-third of the sentence imposed. The sentencing court could also fix the maximum sentence to be served, at which point the inmate could be released on parole. 18 U.S.C. §§4205(a) and 4205(b), as it was in effect before being repealed by section 218(a) of P.L. 98-473.

---

inmates would be eligible for parole consideration.[124] It would appear likely that the commission and the U.S. Probation and Pretrial Services office would need increased resources in order to properly manage what would likely be a significant increase in their caseloads.

There might be some concern about whether allowing federal inmates to be released on parole would pose a threat to public safety. Concerns about recidivism are not unfounded. Research published by the Bureau of Justice Statistics found that over two-thirds (67.5%) of inmates released in 1994 were rearrested within three years and nearly half (46.9%) were convicted for a new crime.[125] While the data are dated, this remains one of the most comprehensive studies on recidivism. Concerns about offenders committing new crimes while on parole have led some jurisdictions to implement intensive supervision programs where parolees are subject to more rigorous conditions of release and more frequent contacts with a parole officer. While intensive supervision programs might in theory reduce the likelihood that parolees commit new offenses while in the community, the body of research on intensive supervision programs suggests that these programs do not reduce recidivism.[126] Depending on how recidivism is defined, intensive supervision programs may actually increase "recidivism" because they are more likely to detect technical violations of the conditions of release.[127] This can create a paradox for policymakers: parole might be considered as a means of reducing the prison population, but it might actually increase the number of inmates in prisons as more return to prison for violating the conditions of parole. Should Congress choose to reinstate parole, policymakers might consider evidence-based measures so that parole helps as many inmates successfully transition back into the community as possible. The options Congress could consider are similar to those outlined above for successful probation programs, namely

- using a validated risk assessment tool to sort parolees into high- and low-risk groups;

- ensuring that parolees with a demonstrated need for rehabilitative programming have access to evidence-based, appropriately delivered programs;

- requiring parolees who violate their conditions of release to serve intermediate sanctions rather than returning them to prison; and

- allowing parolees who strictly adhere to the conditions of their parole to be released early.

Also, like probationers, data indicate that parolees are at the highest risk for recidivism during their first year of parole.[128] This suggests that in order to decrease the risk of recidivism services should be more intensive during the parolee's first year on release. Some research suggests that

---

[124] Data provided by the U.S. Department of Justice, Bureau of Prisons.

[125] Patrick A. Langan and David J. Levin, United States Department of Justice, Bureau of Justice Statistics, *Recidivism of Prisoners Released in 1994*, Report NCJ193427, June 2002. For a summary of this study and other studies on recidivism, see CRS Report RL34287, *Offender Reentry: Correctional Statistics, Reintegration into the Community, and Recidivism*, by Nathan James.

[126] Doris Layton MacKenzie, *What Works in Corrections: Reducing the Criminal Activities of Offenders and Delinquents* (New York: Cambridge University Press, 2006), p. 310.

[127] Ibid.

[128] Community Corrections: Probation, Parole, and Prisoner Reentry, p. 524.

intensive supervision programs can reduce recidivism when they are combined with treatment and rehabilitative programming.[129]

Expanding Good Time Credits

Another potential policy option Congress could consider as a means to slow the growth of, or possibly reduce, the federal prison population is to expand the BOP's authority to grant good time credit to inmates. As outlined above, Congress abolished parole for federal inmates in the 1980s, which means that inmates cannot be released before serving their entire sentence, minus any good time credit, even if the inmate's risk of recidivism is low. Under current law, the BOP can grant up to 54 days of good time credit per year to inmates serving a sentence of more than one year, assuming the inmate has demonstrated "exemplary compliance with institutional disciplinary regulations" and is making satisfactory progress on completing a GED (assuming the inmate does not have a GED or a high school diploma).[130]

In addition to the amount of good time credit an inmate can earn, the BOP is allowed to reduce a non-violent inmate's sentence by up to one year if the inmate participates in residential substance abuse treatment.[131] It has been argued that teaming good time credit with a program that places inmates with objectively assessed needs and risks in evidence-based programs to address those needs and risks can reduce recidivism and cut prison costs.[132] Congress could consider allowing the BOP to award good time credit for inmates who have a need for and successfully complete rehabilitative programs other than residential drug abuse treatment. However, expanding good time credit for participation in rehabilitative programming would likely require Congress, at least in the short term, to expand funding for rehabilitative programs and inmate skills and needs assessments. While expanding current good time credit policies might help reduce prison overcrowding, there might be some concern that the BOP would effectively be reducing inmates' sentences without the sentencing court's approval. Additional good time credit would also allow inmates to be released before serving a significant (85%) portion of their sentence, a key rationale for why parole was eliminated in the first place. In addition, some may feel that regardless of an inmate's efforts to rehabilitate himself or herself or the risk he or she would pose to society when released, the inmate was sent to prison as a punishment for a crime, hence the inmate should serve his or her full sentence.

Sentence Reduction

In addition to allowing the BOP to grant more good time credit to inmates, Congress could also consider whether to amend the conditions under which courts can reduce an inmate's sentence. Under current law (18 U.S.C. §3582(c)(1)(A)), the BOP can petition the court to reduce an inmate's sentence if the court finds that "extraordinary and compelling reasons warrant such a reduction"; or the inmate is at least 70 years of age, has served at least 30 years of his or her sentence, and a determination has been made by the Director of the BOP that the inmate is not a

---

[129] Doris Layton MacKenzie, *What Works in Corrections: Reducing the Criminal Activities of Offenders and Delinquents* (New York: Cambridge University Press, 2006), p. 318.

[130] 18 U.S.C. §3624(b)(1).

[131] 18 U.S.C. §3621(e)(2)(B).

[132] Dora Schriro, "Is Good Time a Good Idea? A Practitioner's Perspective," *The Federal Sentencing Reporter*, vol. 21, no. 3 (February 2009), p. 181.

danger to the safety of any other person or the community. Congress required the USSC, when issuing a policy statement regarding sentence modification under 18 U.S.C. §3582(c)(1)(A), to "describe what should be considered extraordinary and compelling reasons for sentence reduction, including the criteria to be applied and a list of specific examples."[133] Under §1B1.13 of the U.S. Sentencing Guidelines, the USSC deemed the following circumstances to be "extraordinary and compelling reasons" for a sentence reduction:

- The inmate is suffering from a terminal illness.

- The inmate is suffering from a permanent physical or medical condition, or is experiencing deteriorating physical or mental health because of the aging process, that substantially diminishes the ability of the defendant to provide self-care within the environment of a correctional facility and for which conventional treatment promises no substantial improvement.

- The death or incapacitation of the inmate's only family member capable of caring for the inmate's minor child or minor children.

- As determined by the Director of the BOP, there exists in the inmate's case an extraordinary and compelling reason other than, or in combination with, the reasons described above.

Pursuant to 28 U.S.C. §944(t), rehabilitation of an inmate is not, by itself, an extraordinary and compelling reason for granting a sentence reduction. If the court grants a sentence reduction under 18 U.S.C. §3582(c)(1)(A), the court is also allowed to impose a term of probation or supervised release, with or without conditions, for a period up to the amount of time that was remaining on the inmate's sentence.

One of the critiques of this program is that it relies on the BOP to petition the court for a review of an inmate's sentence. One commentator argues that the BOP narrowly interprets when inmates should be allowed to apply for a sentence reduction, effectively limiting applications to cases where the inmate is terminally ill and near death.[134] The regulations governing the program do not state that consideration for a sentence reduction under this program will be limited to cases where the inmate is terminally ill, but it does state that consideration for a sentence reduction under 18 U.S.C. §3582(c)(1)(A) is limited to "particularly extraordinary or compelling circumstances which could not reasonably have been foreseen by the court at the time of sentencing."[135]

Congress could consider modifications to the requirements for sentence reduction under 18 U.S.C. §3582(c)(1)(A) to allow more inmates to have their sentences reduced. For example, Congress could consider allowing courts to consider rehabilitation—either as an extraordinary and compelling reason on its own, or in consort with other reasons—when making determinations about sentence reductions. Expanding the authority of courts to grant a sentence reduction could allow inmates deemed to be a low threat to public safety to be placed in the community earlier, thereby freeing up bedspace in federal prisons.

---

[133] 28 U.S.C. §994(t).

[134] Stephen R. Sady, "Second Look Resentencing under 18 U.S.C. §3582(c) as an Example of Bureau of Prisons Policies That Result in Overincarceration," *Federal Sentencing Reporter*, vol. 21, no. 3 (February 2009), p. 167.

[135] 28 C.F.R. §571.60.

An inmate granted a sentence reduction could still be required to serve a term of supervised release, which would allow federal probation officers to monitor the inmate after he or she is released, a possible advantage over allowing inmates to be released early by increasing good conduct time. However, it is likely that the judicial branch would require additional resources in order to process more applications for sentence reductions under the program and properly monitor inmates whose sentences were reduced but who were placed on supervised release. Also, there might be a question as to whether this would turn the courts into de facto parole boards. Congress eliminated parole in the federal system, in part, over concerns that inmates were incarcerated for less than an appropriate amount of time and disparities in decisions over who received parole. Under this possible system, inmates could be released before serving a majority of their sentences, but Congress could address this concern by not allowing inmates to be eligible for a sentence reduction until they have served a certain portion of their entire sentence.

A potentially more difficult issue for Congress to address is how judges would make decisions if granted broader authority to reduce sentences under the program. It is possible that an inmate's opportunity to receive a sentence reduction would depend on which judge ruled on the inmate's petition. This concern mirrors some of the concerns that existed about how much sway parole boards held over who was granted parole.

Congress could also consider amending the requirements under 18 U.S.C. §3582(c)(1)(A) so that inmates could be released before turning 70. Research indicates that most offenders "age-out" of crime; that is, the older offenders get, the less likely they are to commit new crimes.[136] It appears likely that more elderly inmates could safely be released from confinement and placed on home confinement for the remainder of their sentences.[137] However, the data show that granting early release to elderly offenders would only have a minimal effect on prison overcrowding. In FY2010, approximately 14% were over the age of 50 and about 4% of inmates were over the age of 60.[138] In addition, while elderly inmates might pose a reduced threat to public safety, there is

---

[136] Lindsey Devers, *Desistance and Developmental Life Course Theories: Research Summary*, U.S. Department of Justice, Office of Justice Programs, Bureau of Justice Assistance, Washington, DC, November 9, 2011, p. 7, http://www.ojp.usdoj.gov/BJA/pdf/DesistanceResearchSummary.pdf.

[137] Under section 231(g) of the Second Chance Act of 2007 (P.L. 110-199), the BOP was directed to conduct a pilot program in FY2009 and FY2010 whereby eligible inmates would be placed on home confinement for the remainder of their sentences. Inmates eligible to participate in the pilot program were 65 or older; non-violent or non-sex offenders; not serving a life sentence; severed the greater of 10 years or 75% of their sentences; did not have a history of escape or escape attempts; and were determined to not be at risk for recidivism. The Government Accountability Office (GAO) reported that of the 855 inmates who applied for the pilot program, 71 (8.3%) were determined by the BOP to have met the criteria for the program and were eventually placed on home confinement. The GAO noted that as of June 2012, none of the inmates placed on home confinement had recidivated or violated the terms of release. However, the BOP reported that it did not save any money by placing elderly inmates on home confinement; in fact, the BOP reported that it cost approximately $540,000 more to place the inmates on home confinement. The GAO contends that the BOP's conclusions might not be a reliable indicator of the potential cost of the program should it be continued or expanded. First, while the BOP knows what it paid RRCs to monitor inmates placed on home confinement, the BOP does not know the exact cost of home confinement. The BOP negotiates with RRCs to provide supervision of inmates placed on home confinement. RRCs are paid a per diem rate to house an inmate and they are paid 50% of the per diem rate to supervise an inmate placed on home confinement. However, the BOP does not require RRC contractors to separate the cost of home confinement services and RRCs bedspace, so the BOP does not actually know the cost of home confinement. Second, some of the costs of the pilot program would have been incurred regardless because the BOP is currently authorized to place all of the inmates in the program on home confinement for up to six months. Government Accountability Office, *Federal Bureau of Prisons: Methods for Estimating Incarceration and Community Corrections Costs and Results of the Elderly Offender Pilot*, GAO-12-807R, Washington, DC, July 27, 2012, http://www.gao.gov/assets/600/593089.pdf.

[138] Data from the U.S. Department of Justice, Office of Justice Programs, Bureau of Justice Statistics, *Federal Criminal* (continued...)

---

likely to be some sentiment that any offender, regardless of age and safety risk, should serve his or her entire sentence.

Modifying the "Safety Valve" Provision

There are other potential amendments to the criminal code Congress could consider if policymakers wanted to potentially reduce the size of the federal prison population. For example, Congress could consider expanding the "safety valve" provision under 18 U.S.C. §3553(f). The safety valve provision allows judges to impose a sentence without regard to the mandatory minimum sentences for certain drug offenses[139] if the following conditions are met:

- The defendant does not have more than one criminal history point, as determined under the sentencing guidelines.

- The defendant did not use violence or credible threats of violence or possess a firearm or other dangerous weapon (or induce another participant to do so) in connection with the offense.

- The offense did not result in death or serious bodily injury to any person.

- The defendant was not an organizer, leader, manager, or supervisor of others in the offense, as determined by the sentencing guidelines, and was not engaged in a continuing criminal enterprise.

- No later than the time of the sentencing hearing, the defendant has truthfully provided to the government all information and evidence the defendant has concerning the offense or offenses that were part of the same course of conduct or of a common scheme or plan, but the fact that the defendant has no relevant or useful or other information to provide or that the government is already aware of the information shall not preclude a determination by the court that the defendant has not complied with the requirements of the provision.

Currently, the safety valve provision cannot be applied to defendants facing a mandatory minimum sentence for an offense that is not drug-related. The safety valve provision was enacted after Congress became concerned that the mandatory minimum sentencing provisions could result in equally severe penalties for both the more and the less culpable offenders.[140] Congress could consider expanding the provision so that it would apply to defendants facing mandatory minimum sentences for offenses other than drug crimes. This option would allow Congress to retain mandatory minimum penalties that can still be applied to more serious offenders while allowing judges to sentence less serious offenders to shorter periods of incarceration.

(...continued)

Case Processing Statistics, http://www.bjs.gov/fjsrc/.

[139] These offenses are trafficking in various controlled substances (21 U.S.C. §841), possession of certain controlled substances (21 U.S.C. §844), attempt or conspiracy to violate controlled substance provisions carrying mandatory minimum sentences (21 U.S.C. §846), smuggling controlled substances in violation of 21 U.S.C. §§952, 953, 955, 957, or 959 (21 U.S.C. §960), and attempt or conspiracy to violate the controlled substance import/export provisions (21 U.S.C. §963).

[140] CRS Report R41326, *Federal Mandatory Minimum Sentences: The Safety Valve and Substantial Assistance Exceptions*, by Charles Doyle. See also U.S. Congress, House Committee on the Judiciary, *Mandatory Minimum Sentencing Reform Act of 1994*, to accompany H.R. 3979, 103rd Cong., 2nd sess., March 24, 1994, H.Rept. 103-460 (Washington: GPO, 1994), p. 2.

One idea put forth is to amend current law so that judges could apply the safety valve in instances where the recommended sentencing guideline range is below the mandatory minimum penalty and where the defendant's offense did not result in death or serious bodily injury to anyone and the defendant has provided the government with all information and evidence available to the defendant.[141] Under the proposal, the defendant could not be sentenced to less than the minimum of the sentencing range calculated under the sentencing guidelines. Many of the conditions placed on the current safety valve provision would remain (e.g., not using violence or possessing a weapon and not being an organizer or leader in the offense), but rather than being a bar from being eligible for the safety valve, they would be factors for the court to consider when deciding whether to sentence a defendant below the mandatory minimum penalty. Judges would be required to state for the record why they chose to impose a sentence below the mandatory minimum penalty, and those decisions would be subject to appellate review. However, as noted above, the USSC has incorporated many mandatory minimum sentences into the sentencing guidelines. Therefore, in some instances the guideline sentence might be equal to or exceed the mandatory minimum penalty, which would render the proposed safety valve provision moot. One possible solution to this conundrum would be to allow the USSC to give due consideration to mandatory minimum penalties when formulating the sentencing guidelines, but not requiring the USSC to make the guidelines consistent with mandatory minimum penalties.[142]

Repealing Federal Criminal Statutes for Some Offenses

One of the highlighted reasons for the growth in the federal prison population was the "federalization" of offenses that were traditionally under the sole jurisdiction of state authorities. Policymakers could consider revising the U.S. Code so that federal law enforcement focuses on crimes where states do not have jurisdiction over the offenses or where the federal government is best suited to investigate and prosecute the offenders (e.g., the offense involves multiple individuals acting together to commit crimes across several states). Some crimes will always be federal offenses. For example, the federal government will always be responsible for prosecuting individuals who commit immigration-related offenses because immigration laws are solely the jurisdiction of the federal government. However, over the years the federal government has become more involved in investigating, prosecuting, and incarcerating people who commit drug offenses and offenses where a convicted felon is found to be in possession of a firearm. In many instances, states have criminal penalties for individuals who commit these types of crimes. For example, in his testimony before the House Subcommittee on Crime, Terrorism, and Homeland Security at a hearing on the unintended consequences of mandatory minimum penalties, Eric Sterling, the President of the Criminal Justice Policy Foundation argued

> [f]ederal drug cases should focus exclusively on the international organizations that use their profits from the manufacture and distribution of cocaine, opium and heroin, methamphetamine, and cannabis to finance assassinations, terrorism, wholesale corruption and bribery, organized crime generally, and the destabilization of our allies...Every state in the U.S. has a great capacity to investigate, prosecute and punish the high-level local drug traffickers that operate within their jurisdiction. State and local police and prosecutors outnumber federal agents and prosecutors. State prisons far exceed the capacity of federal prisons...Almost none of the crack [cocaine] dealers that proliferate in countless U.S.

---

[141] Paul G. Cassell and Erik Luna, "Sense and Sensibility in Mandatory Minimum Sentencing," *Federal Sentencing Reporter*, vol. 23, no. 3 (February 2011), p. 222.

[142] Ibid., p. 225.

neighborhoods warrant federal prosecution. There are neighborhood criminals and their crimes are state crimes. If a state's law does not adequately punish a crack [cocaine] dealer, *that is the state's problem. Inadequate state laws do not warrant wasting very scarce, powerful federal resources even on serious neighborhood criminals* [emphasis original].[143]

Scaling back the scope of the federal criminal code could help reduce the size of the federal prison population in the future by reducing the number of people prosecuted and sentenced to incarceration in federal courts. However, this policy option could increase the burden on state criminal justice systems since they would be responsible for prosecuting and incarcerating offenders who are no longer tried in federal courts. By year-end 2011, according to the BJS, 24 state correctional systems were at or above their highest capacity, and another 10 state correctional systems were between 90% and 99% of their highest capacity.[144] Since nearly three-quarters of states have prison systems that are operating at 90% of capacity or higher, it would appear that if the federal government chooses not to prosecute some offenses, thereby leaving states with the responsibility to do so, it would require states to either expand their prison capacities or possibly decline to prosecute some offenses. Also, it is possible that an expansion of state correctional systems could have a significant effect on state finances. The Vera Institute of Justice reported that state correctional spending has nearly quadrupled over the past two decades, which makes it the fasting growing budget item after Medicaid.[145] The National Association of State Budget Officers reported that in FY2011, correctional expenditures accounted for 7.4% of all state general fund expenditures, with a range of 24.3% (Michigan) to 2.9% (Minnesota).[146] Since states typically cannot run a budget deficit, any expansion in correctional expenditures would have to be paid for with cuts to other state services, increased taxes, or issuing bonds.

Conclusion

There are almost 195,000 more inmates incarcerated in federal prisons currently than there were in FY1980, a nearly 790% increase in the federal prison population. The growth in the federal prison population is the result of several changes to the federal criminal justice system, including expanding the use of mandatory minimum penalties; the federal government taking jurisdiction in more criminal cases; and eliminating parole for federal inmates.

The analyses presented in this report show that the BOP faces several challenges resulting from the increasing number of inmates in the federal prison system. First, it is increasingly expensive to operate the federal prison system. Second, the federal prison system is becoming more overcrowded, especially in high- and medium-security male prisons. Third, the cost of caring for more inmates has left the BOP in a position where it might not be able to hire an adequate number

---

[143] Statement of Eric E. Sterling, President of the Criminal Justice Policy Foundation, U.S. Congress, House Committee on the Judiciary, Subcommittee on Crime, Terrorism, and Homeland Security, *Mandatory Minimums and Unintended Consequences*, Hearing on H.R. 2934, H.R. 834 and H.R. 1466, 111th Cong., 1st sess., July 14, 2009, H.Hrg. 111-48 (Washington: GPO, 2010), pp. 114-115.

[144] *Prisoners in 2011*, p. 31.

[145] Christian Henrichson and Ruth Delaney, *The Price of Prisons: What Incarceration Costs Taxpayers*, Vera Institute of Justice, New York, NT, January 2012, p. 2, http://www.vera.org/download?file=3542/ Price%2520of%2520Prisons_updated%2520version_072512.pdf.

[146] National Association of State Budget Officers, *2010 State Expenditure Report: Examining Fiscal 2009-2011 State Spending*, Washington, DC, 2011, p. 56, http://www.nasbo.org/sites/default/files/ 2010%20State%20Expenditure%20Report.pdf.

of staff. Finally, the steady influx of inmates combined with dwindling levels of funding for prison construction and maintenance has placed a strain on the federal prison system's infrastructure.

If Congress moves forward with a debate about prison and sentencing reform, policymakers might also consider whether incarcerating more offenders would continue to generate a significant deterrent effect. Research suggests that while incarceration did contribute to lower violent crime rates in the 1990s, there are declining marginal returns associated with ever-increasing levels of incarceration.[147] The diminishing level of return resulting from higher levels of incarceration might be explained by the fact that higher levels of incarceration are likely to include more offenders who are either at the end of their criminal careers or who were at a low risk of committing crimes at a high rate (so-called "career criminals").[148] Another possible reason for diminishing marginal returns might be that more of the individuals incarcerated over the past three decades have been incarcerated for crimes where there is a high level of replacement.[149] For example, if a serial rapist is incarcerated, not only is there the potential to prevent future sexual assaults that would have been committed by the offender, but it is also probable that no one else will take that offender's place. However, if a drug dealer is incarcerated, it is possible that someone will step in to take that person's place; therefore, no further crimes may be averted by incarcerating the individual.

The unprecedented increase in the federal prison population over the past three decades was not the result of a singular policy change; likewise, it would appear that, should Congress choose to address prison population growth, it would require a multi-faceted approach to reduce the number of federal inmates in any substantive manner. Congress might consider options—such as expanding the capacity of the federal prison system, continued investment in rehabilitative programs, and placing inmates in private prisons—that would either continue or expand current correctional policies. However, Congress might also consider changing or reversing some of the policies that have been put into place over the years which contributed to the increasing number of federal prison inmates. Some of these options include placing some inmates in alternatives to incarceration, such as probation, or expanding early release options by allowing inmates to earn more good time credit or allowing inmates to be placed on parole once again. Congress could consider reducing the amount of time inmates are incarcerated in federal prisons by limiting the number of crimes subject to mandatory minimum penalties or reducing the length of the mandatory minimum sentence. Finally, policymakers could consider allowing states to investigate and prosecute offenses that have become subject to federal jurisdiction over the past three decades.

---

[147] Anne Morrison Piehl and Bert Useem, "Prisons," in *Crime and Public Policy*, ed. Joan Petersilia and James Q. Wilson, 2nd ed. (New York: Oxford University Press, 2011), p. 542.

[148] Doris Layton MacKenzie, "Reducing the Criminal Activities of Known Offenders and Delinquents: Crime Prevention in the Courts and Corrections," in *Evidence-based Crime Prevention*, ed. Lawrence W. Sherman, David P. Farrington, Brandon C. Welsh and Doris Layton MacKenzie (New York: Routledge, 2002), p. 337.

[149] Bert Useem and Anne Morrison Piehl, *Prison State: The Challenge of Mass Incarceration* (New York: Cambridge University Press, 2008), p. 74.

Appendix. Select BOP Data

Table A-1. Appropriations for the BOP by Account; Number of Inmates Under the BOP's Jurisdiction; and the Number and Capacity of and Overcrowding in BOP Facilities

Appropriations amounts are in thousands of dollars

Fiscal Year	Appropriations			Prison Population			Prison Facilities		
	Salaries and Expenses	Buildings and Facilities	Total	Institution	Contract	Total	Number	Capacity	Over-crowding
1980	$323,884	$5,960	$329,844	24,268	372	24,640	41	—	—
1981	351,759	10,020	361,779	26,195	118	26,313	43	23,648[a]	11%[a]
1982	378,016	56,481	434,497	28,133	2,398	30,531	43	24,072[a]	17%[a]
1983	412,133	66,667	478,800	30,214	3,002	33,216	43	23,936[a]	26%[a]
1984	464,850	47,711	512,561	32,317	3,478	35,795	43	24,874[a]	30%[a]
1985	536,932	86,043	622,975	36,001	4,329	40,330	46	25,532[a]	41%[a]
1986	561,480	44,082	605,562	41,506	4,549	46,055	47	27,785[a]	49%[a]
1987	656,941	219,249	876,190	44,194	5,184	49,378	47	27,854[a]	59%[a]
1988	772,013	297,076	1,069,089	44,142	6,371	50,513	52	28,143[a]	57%[a]
1989	962,016	612,914	1,574,930	51,153	6,609	57,762	58	31,727[a]	61%[a]
1990	1,138,778	1,511,953	2,650,731	58,021	6,915	64,936	64	34,239[a]	69%[a]
1991	1,363,645	374,358	1,738,003	64,131	7,377	71,508	68	42,531	51%
1992	1,649,121	462,090	2,111,211	70,670	9,008	79,678	69	48,527	46%
1993	1,793,470	339,225	2,132,695	79,799	8,766	88,565	72	57,610	39%
1994	1,962,605	269,543	2,232,148	85,850	9,312	95,162	75	64,751	33%
1995	2,319,722	276,301	2,596,023	90,159	10,799	100,958	83	72,039	25%
1996	2,546,893[b]	334,728	2,881,621	94,695	10,748	105,443	86	76,442	24%
1997	2,748,427[c]	435,200	3,183,627	101,091	11,198	112,289	91	83,022	22%
1998	2,847,777[d]	255,133	3,102,910	108,207	14,109	122,316	92	86,051	26%
1999	2,888,853[e]	410,997	3,299,850	117,295	16,394	133,689	94	89,581	31%
2000	3,111,073[f]	556,780	3,667,853	125,560	19,565	145,125	97	94,927	32%
2001	3,469,739	833,822	4,303,561	130,327	26,245	156,572	100	98,425	32%
2002	3,805,118	807,808	4,612,926	137,527	25,909	163,436	102	103,262	33%
2003	4,044,788	396,632	4,441,420	146,212	26,287	172,499	103	105,193	39%
2004	4,414,313	393,515	4,807,828	152,518	27,377	179,895	109	108,537	41%
2005	4,571,385	205,076	4,776,461	159,501	27,893	187,394	116	118,652	34%
2006	4,830,160	99,961	4,930,121	162,514	30,070	192,584	114[g]	119,510	36%
2007	5,012,433	432,425	5,444,858	167,323	32,697	200,020	114	122,189	37%
2008	5,346,740	372,720	5,719,460	165,964	35,704	201,668	114	122,366	36%

Fiscal Year	Appropriations			Prison Population			Prison Facilities		
	Salaries and Expenses	Buildings and Facilities	Total	Institution	Contract	Total	Number	Capacity	Over-crowding
2009	5,600,792	575,807	6,176,599	172,423	36,336	208,759	115	125,778	37%
2010	6,106,231	99,155	6,205,386	173,289	36,938	210,227	116	126,713	37%
2011	6,282,410	98,957	6,381,367	177,934	39,834	217,768	117	127,795	39%
2012	6,551,281	90,000	6,641,281	177,556	41,131	218,687	118	128,359	38%

Source: U.S. Department of Justice, Bureau of Prisons.

Notes: The BOP did not provide capacity and overcrowding data for FY1980. Appropriation amounts in **Table A-1** include all supplemental and reprogrammed appropriations and any rescissions of enacted budget authority, but they *do not* include rescissions of *unobligated balances*. From FY1980 to FY1995, funding for the National Institute of Corrections (NIC) was included in a separate account. Since FY1996, funding for the NIC has been included in the S&E account. Funding for the NIC for FY1980-FY1995 was added to the S&E account to make funding for the S&E account comparable across fiscal years.

a.   Capacity and overcrowding were calculated based on single cell occupancy

b.   Includes $13.5 million appropriated from the Violent Crime Reduction Trust Fund.

c.   Includes $25.2 million appropriated from the Violent Crime Reduction Trust Fund.

d.   Includes $26.1 million appropriated from the Violent Crime Reduction Trust Fund.

e.   Includes $26.5 million appropriated from the Violent Crime Reduction Trust Fund.

f.   Includes $22.5 million appropriated from the Violent Crime Reduction Trust Fund.

g.   In FY2006, the BOP closed four stand-alone prison camps and activated two new prisons.

Table A-2. Appropriations for the BOP, by Decision Unit, FY1999-FY2012

Appropriations in thousands of dollars

Fiscal Year	Salaries and Expenses				Buildings and Facilities	
	Inmate Care and Programs	Institution Security and Administration	Contract Confinement	Management and Administration	New Construction	Modernization and Repair
1999	$1,090,148	$1,401,349	$255,062	$142,249	$322,963	$88,034
2000	1,123,856	1,494,809	344,773	147,635	441,003	115,777
2001	1,208,480	1,601,518	511,579	148,162	710,816	123,006
2002	1,311,335	1,722,567	620,145	151,071	675,040	132,768
2003	1,454,481	1,868,538	567,365	154,404	262,956	133,676
2004	1,624,308	2,050,417	574,473	165,115	177,620	164,000
2005	1,682,656	2,094,917	627,135	166,677	25,372	179,704
2006	1,740,011	2,227,223	683,031	179,895	48,115	51,846
2007	1,774,048	2,297,055	757,851	183,479	368,875	63,550
2008	1,942,077	2,409,112	814,529	181,022	302,720	70,000
2009	2,070,002	2,495,196	840,933	194,661	465,180	110,627
2010	2,215,992	2,708,651	981,112	200,476	25,386	73,769
2011	2,294,174	2,783,664	996,772	207,800	25,335	73,622
2012	2,421,272	2,880,290	1,040,213	209,506	23,035	66,695

Source: U.S. Department of Justice, Bureau of Prisons.

Notes: Amounts in **Table A-2** include all supplemental and reprogrammed appropriations and any rescissions of enacted budget authority, but they *do not* include rescissions of *unobligated balances*.

Author Contact Information

Nathan James
Analyst in Crime Policy
njames@crs.loc.gov, 7-0264

www.ingramcontent.com/pod-product-compliance
Lightning Source LLC
Chambersburg PA
CBHW081225170526
45165CB00009B/2961